595

S·T·Y·L·I·S·H
KNITTING

from handspun or commercial yarns

S·T·Y·L·I·S·H
KNITTING

from handspin or commercial yarns

Nina Shuttlewood

•

B.T. Batsford Ltd, London

To my husband, James, who has never stopped
believing in me and is *still* giving unfailing
encouragement.

First published 1988
© Nina Shuttlewood 1988

ISBN 0 7134 5167 X

Typeset by Tek-Art Ltd, Kent
and printed in Great Britain by
Bath Press Ltd
Bath, Avon
for the publishers
B.T. Batsford Ltd
4 Fitzhardinge Street
London W1H 0AH

CONTENTS

Acknowledgements

I should like to thank the following: Mabel Ross for allowing me to use the 'Mabel Ross System'; Mark Gilder of Braintree, Essex, for the photography; David Songer for his photograph of yarn; Diane Hall, Juliet Smith, Richard Embling and Joe Embling for modelling the garments; all my hard-working knitters, and a special thank you to Peter and Diane Hall for the use of their lovely home.

Spinning your own yarn is the most exciting and rewarding craft. Sooner or later, as you progress in expertise, you will want to look at the fashion yarns on the wool shop shelf and know how to create the same.

The easiest way of moving into creative and textured yarn design is first to understand and know your plys as most of the yarns are spun in the normal way and the textures are made up in the plying. So it is worth while spending some time knowing how to make a 3-ply, 4-ply or double knitting yarn with confidence.

By using the 'Mabel Ross System' all knitters, using both hand spun and commercial yarns, will easily be able to work out how many threads per centimetre/inch will be needed to arrive at the thickness of the yarn needed for the garment they intend to knit.

This book will show you not only how to spin the yarn at the required thickness but, by going into 'The Mabel Ross Advanced System', show you how to spin at the right degree for spinning and again for plying for a lovely balanced yarn. This is done by what is called controlled spinning, which is a means of feeding in the fibres at the necessary thickness, and at the right length every time your foot treadles; then no matter whether the spinning is done all at once or at yearly intervals on repeat spinning, the yarn will always be identical.

The textures of most of the yarns are done in the plying and by working to a set spinning instruction for that yarn. Then when we are treacling for our knop, pushing for our bouclé or wrapping for our slub the mystery has been taken out of the final result. You will know that by following the spinning instructions on each and every garment and each and every yarn, good results are always available.

WHEEL RATIOS

It is vital to know your own spinning wheel ratio in order to obtain accurate results without any difficulty. The easiest method to find out your wheel ratio is to tie a piece of yarn on to the top bar of your spinning wheel (see fig. 1). Now with the hands on the flyer count the number of *complete turns* you are able to make with the flyer before the bar with the yarn attached to it arrives back at the top of the wheel again.

If the flyer twisted six-and-a-half times then the wheel ratio is six-and-a-half to one or $6\frac{1}{2}$:1. This is the figure *always* to look for in your spinning and plying instructions; *ignore any other instructions*.

The same will apply if you should use a different wheel. First check the ratio (which this time may be 5:1), then whilst using that wheel follow the spinning and plying instructions under the 5:1 ratio.

The Ashford spinning wheels are very popular. The Standard has a wheel ratio of $6\frac{1}{2}$:1, but the Traveller is $5\frac{1}{2}$:1; whichever wheel you use, just follow the ratio instructions for that wheel and you will make identical yarns! It really works – have two or three of your friends with different wheel ratios spin the instructions for a garment such as *Grace* or *Joan*. We note that for 2-ply yarn the thickness of the threads is 45 threads per inch; under the wheel ratio 5:1 the fibres are fed into the spinning wheel $\frac{1}{2}$ in. every treadle, whereas for a 9:1 ratio, the feed in is 1 in. for every treadle. The same is for plying. For every 18 in. of yarn to be plyed, the ratio of 5:1 will need to put in 18 treadles into the yarn before feeding it into the orifice, whereas the ratio 9:1 will only do 9 treadles. Nevertheless the yarns when complete *will be identical*. By following your wheel ratio you will get a good balanced yarn. (For metric measurements please refer to conversion table on page 130.)

FEED IN

Feed in means nothing more than learning to spin by treadling in a rhythm. As the foot goes down on the treadle (see fig. 2), pull out, say, 1 in. of fibres; as the foot comes up (see fig. 3) let those fibres into the orifice, and so on – *all*

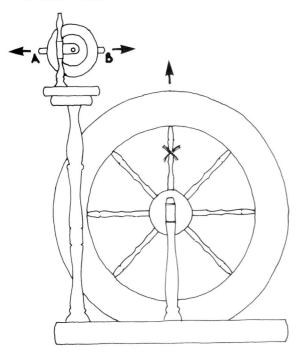

1a *Tie piece of yarn on to the top bar of the spinning wheel*

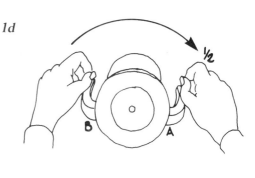

1d

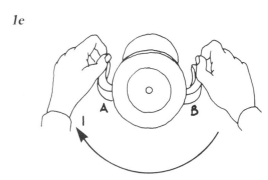

1e

1b,c,d,e *With hands on flyer count number of complete turns you are able to make before bar with yarn arrives back at the top of the wheel again*

1b

1c

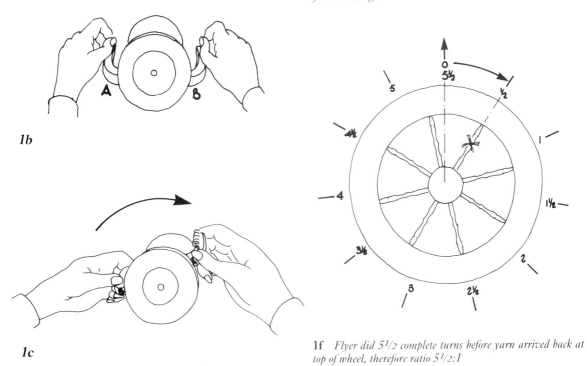

1f *Flyer did 5 1/2 complete turns before yarn arrived back at top of wheel, therefore ratio 5 1/2:1*

the time. After a while, like anything else that has been practised, you wonder how you spun in the first place. But the feed in and rhythmic treadling is important and needs to be practised.

It may be a good idea at this stage to make yourself a card for measuring your feed in rate of, say, 6 in. in length. Mark off the inches on this card by colouring in every other inch with a coloured pen. Mark the first, second and third inches into half inches. When spinning instructions give you a feed in of 1 in., 1½ in. or 2 in. per treadle, simply lay the card on your lap and move your hands to the 1, 1½ or 2 in. marker on the card. Trying to guess the measurement may result in the feed in getting wider or shorter, but the constant reminder on your lap will keep you accurate.

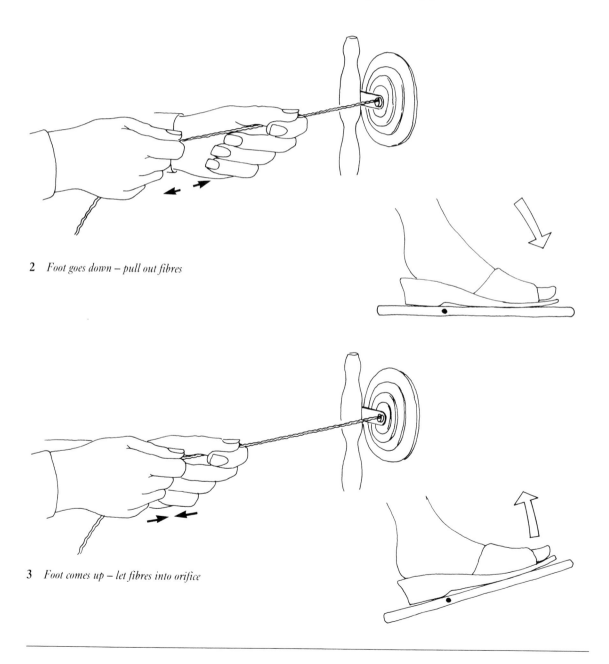

2   *Foot goes down – pull out fibres*

3   *Foot comes up – let fibres into orifice*

PREPARATION OF FIBRES

In order to move freely through your fibres at each treadle, preparation is all-important. In fact, I cannot stress too strongly the need for good preparation, for then fibres will just flow onto the wheel (see fig. 4).

A badly made rolag or roving will result in an enforced stop to correct it; then, perhaps, without thinking you may continue to treadle whilst correcting it and destroy the balance of your yarn.

The next important thing is to treadle *slowly* at all times. If you have any problems, stop treadling, sort it out and recommence treadling.

Remember that spinning is supposed to be a therapeutic craft!

CARDING

Your hand carders are a very valuable asset to your spinning equipment.

Always try and work through your fleece methodically and neatly, laying staples tidily along the carders ready for combing (see fig. 5). Your fleece will go so much further than by just pulling a handful of fibres and cramming them onto your carders, so again remember that good preparation means good spinning.

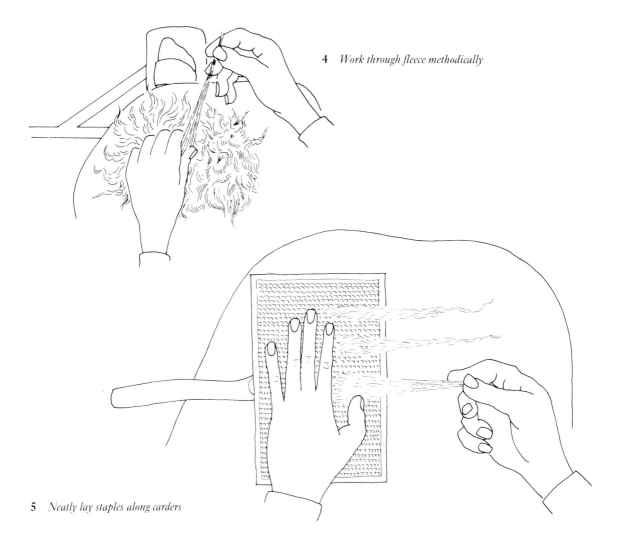

4   *Work through fleece methodically*

5   *Neatly lay staples along carders*

The Mabel Ross system

To spin yarn for any particular pattern and produce the desired handknitted garment exactly it is essential that yarn of the correct thickness is spun. A simple method of measuring yarn thickness is illustrated in figs 6 and 7.

Spin a little yarn; now pull back a length from the bobbin. Using a small rod or pencil wind the yarn round it for 1 in., carefully observing the correct direction of winding, as illustrated, so the yarn is not untwisted as you wind it. The successive circuits of the thread should lie close

together, as shown, but not be packed forcibly.

Count the number of threads covering 1 in. and you have a measure of the thread thickness. (If using metric measure cover a minimum of 2 cm and divide the resulting number of threads by 2 to arrive at the correct threads-per-centimetre measure.)

If the thread thickness is not as desired, adjust as you spin, drawing out fibres further for a thinner thread, giving more threads per inch, or, for a thicker thread, draw fibres out less. Once correct thickness is achieved, break off a

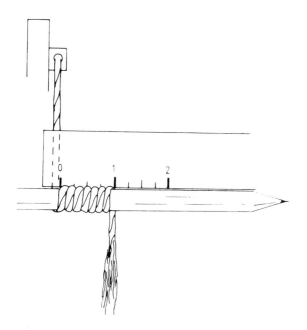

6 *Measuring the thread thickness for Z twist*

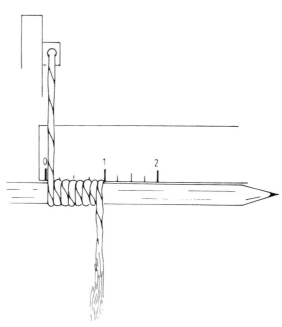

7 *Measuring the thread thickness for S twist*

length of a good sample, tie in a loop (to keep the twist), and keep handy for reference.

The table below enables yarn similar to any commercial yarn to be spun by the hand-spinner. It lists, in column 1, the main basic types of commercial yarns from 2-ply to chunky. Columns 2 and 3 give the approximate thickness of these yarns, measured as threads per inch and also threads per centimetre. Columns 4, 5 and 6 give the size of the knitting needles (in British, metric and American sizing) commonly, though not invariably, used for that yarn. Finally, columns 7 and 8 list the thickness (threads per inch and centimetre) of the singles yarn which should be spun, which, when it is 2-plyed, will be similar in thickness to that of the corresponding commercial yarn.

NOTE

If you wish for a 3-ply yarn for any reason, then your singles must be *half* the thickness of the final yarn required.

The Mabel Ross System

1	2	3	4	5	6	7	8
Commercial yarn type	No. of threads per in.	No. of threads per cm	Appropriate average knitting pin size			Required hand spun singles which when 2-plyed will give equivalent to commercial	
			British	Metric	American	No. of threads per in.	No. of threads per cm
2-ply fingering	25	10	13	2	0	45	18
3-ply fingering	19	7.5	12/11	2.5	1/2	35	14
4-ply fingering	16	6.5	10	3.0	3	27	11
Double Knitting (thin)	14	5.5	9	3.5	4	25	10
Double Knitting (thick)	12	5.0	8	4.0	5	22	9
Aran (thin)	11	4.5	7	4.5	6	20	8
Aran (thick)	10	4.0	6/5	5.0	7/8	17	7
Double-Double	9	3.5	5/4	5.5/6.0	8/9	15	6
Chunky	7/8	3.0	3/2	6/7	10/10½	13	5.5
6-ply rug	5	2.0				9	3.5

Controlled yarns

GRACE

Breed: Shetland
Category: Shortwool and Down

There is nothing quite like the pleasure of slipping into a wool dress, and this finely knitted elegant evening dress, worn with matching hip sash and headband, is no exception. The hip sash can also be used as a stole.

MATERIALS

Handspun
18 threads per cm – single ply
45 threads per in. – single ply

Commercial equivalent – 2-ply
10 threads per cm
25 threads per in.

Handspun yarn
400 (425:425) g Shetland

Commercial yarn
16(17:18) x 25 g balls of Sunbeam 2-ply pure new wool.

Pair 2¼ mm (13) needles
2¼ mm (13) circular needle 100 cm long
Sequins and beads to decorate

MEASUREMENTS

To fit bust 87(92:97) cm [34(36:38) in.]
Length of dress 115 cm [45 in.] adjustable
Sleeve seam 46(47:48) cm [18(18½:19¼) in.]

TENSION

42 sts and 56 rows to 10 cm [4 in.] measured over patt on 2½ mm needles.

ARROWHEAD LACE PATTERN

1st row With RS facing, K1, * (yf,Sl1,K1,psso) twice, K1, (K2tog,yf) twice, K1, rep from * to end.
2nd and 4th rows P.
3rd row K2, * yf, Sl1, K1, psso, yf, Sl1, K2tog, psso, yf, K2tog, yf, K3, rep from * to last 9 sts, yf, Sl1, K1, psso, yf, Sl1, K2tog, psso, yf, K2tog, yf, K2.
These four rows form patt.

DOUBLE MOSS STITCH PATTERN

1st row K1, * P1, K1, rep from * to end.
2nd row P1, * K1, P1, rep from * to end.
3rd row As 2nd row.
4th row As 1st row.
These four rows form patt.

2-ply

SPINNING INSTRUCTIONS													
Wheel Ratio	3:1	3½:1	4:1	4½:1	5:1	5½:1	6:1	6½:1	7:1	8:1	9:1	10:1	12:1
'Feed in' in inches per treadle					½	½-¾	½-¾	½-¾	¾	¾	1	1	1¼
PLYING INSTRUCTIONS													
Per treadles per 18 inches					18	15	15	15	12	12	9	9	8

GRACE

BACK

With 2¼ mm needles cast on 211(221:231)sts and work in arrowhead lace patt for 25 cm [10 in.] *.
Change to double moss stitch patt and cont in patt until work measures 92 cm [36 in.] from beg. (Adjust length here.)
Work one row.
Next row Patt 105(110:115)sts. Leave rem sts on a spare needle.
Cont in patt, dec 1 st on neck edge every other row until work measures 112 cm [44 in.].

Shape shoulders

Keeping patt straight cast off 12(12:15)sts on next and every alternate row until all sts have been cast off.
Rejoin yarn to rem 106(111:116)sts and work as for right side reversing all shapings.

FRONT

Work as for back to *.
Cont in double moss stitch patt until work measures 112 cm [44 in.].
Next row Work 35(40:45)sts. Cast off 140 sts. Leave rem sts on spare needle.

Shape shoulders

(left side)
* Cast off 12(13:15)sts on shoulder edge. Work to last two sts, K2tog at neck edge. *
Work 1 row.
Rep from * to * once more.
Cast off rem sts.
Complete right side to match, reversing shapings.

SLEEVES

With 2¼ mm needles, cast on 101(111:111)sts. Work in arrowhead lace stitch patt for 15 cm [6 in.].
Change to double moss stitch patt increasing 1 st at each end of next and every 4th row until work measures 46(47:48) cm [18(18½:19¼) in.].
Cast off.

TO MAKE UP

Join shoulder seams.
Set in sleeves.
Sew up right-hand side of dress seam. On the left-hand side leave the seam open for all of the arrowhead lace patt 25 cm [10 in.]. Sew up rest of seam.

NECK

With 2¼ mm circular needle pick up 114 sts from right side of back, 114 sts across front of neck and 114 sts down left side of back.
Work in K1, P1 rib for 2 cm [¾ in.] at the same time dec 1 st each side of the V at back of dress to form point. Cast off loosely in rib. Decorate dress with beads and sequins.

SASH

See instructions for *Grace*.
Decorate with beads and sequins.

HEADBAND

Using 2¼ mm needles cast on 230 sts and work in moss st for 6.5 cm [2½ in.]. Cast off in rib.
Decorate with drop pearl beads.

JOAN

Breed: Shetland
Category: Shortwool and Down

A charming stole or snood to be worn with your favourite dress or perhaps even as a sash for the waist or hips to add chic to *Grace*.

Spinning and plying instructions as for *Grace* (p. 15).

MATERIALS

Handspun yarn
150 g Shetland

Commercial yarn
5 x 25 g balls of Sunbeam 2-ply pure new wool.

Pair 2¼ mm (13) needles
Sequins and beads to decorate

MEASUREMENTS

Stole or hip sash 178 cm [70 in.]
Waist sash 127 cm [50 in.]

With 2¼ mm needles cast on 121 sts and work in arrowhead lace stitch patt for required length. Cast off in patt.
   If it is to be used as a hip or waist sash as an accessory to *Grace*, decorate with beads and sequins.

JOAN

EVE

EVE

Breed: Shetland
Category: Shortwool and Down
Other fibre: Silk

Wool and silk two-piece suit. A clever way of making a very attractive sweater into a two-piece suit is by creating a knitted border in the same ribboned pattern as the sweater and sewing it to the bottom of an A-line skirt.

MATERIALS

Handspun – Shetland
14 threads per cm – single ply
35 threads per in. – single ply

Handspun – silk
14 threads per cm – single ply
35 threads per in. – single ply

Commercial equivalent – 3-ply
7.5 threads per cm
19 threads per in.

Handspun yarn
150(200) g white Shetland
200(200) g white cultivated silk

Commercial yarn
12(14) x 25 g balls of Sunbeam 3-ply pure new wool.

Approximately 63(65) m [69(71) yards] 3 mm double-faced satin ribbon
5 small pearl buttons
Pair each 3 mm (11) and 3¾ mm (9) knitting needles

MEASUREMENTS

To fit bust 87-97 cm [34-38 in.]
Length from top of shoulder 54 cm [21¼ in.]
Sleeve seam 21 cm [8¼ in.]

TENSION

28 sts and 38 rows to 10 cm [4 in.] measured over pattern on 3¾ mm needles.

Special instructions
Do not twist or pull ribbon tight.

PATTERN

1st row With WS facing, K.
2nd row P.
3rd row P3, * using ribbon, P1 winding ribbon *twice* round needle, using yarn P2, rep from * to end.
4th row Using yarn knit to ribbon stitch, * slip ribbon stitch purlwise allowing extra loop to fall from needle, K2, rep from * to end.
5th row Using yarn purl to ribbon stitch, * slip ribbon stitch purlwise, P2, rep from * to end.
6th row Using yarn, knit to ribbon stitch, * drop ribbon stitch off needle and leave in front of work, using yarn knit the next 2 sts, pick up the dropped ribbon stitch and knit into the back of the ribbon stitch, rep from * to end.
7th row P.
8th–12th rows K.
These 12 rows form pattern.

BACK AND FRONT (both alike)

With 3 mm knitting needles cast on 120 sts.
K1, P1 rib for 8 cm [3¼ in.].
Change to 3¾ mm needles and proceed in pattern for 32 cm [12½ in.].

3-ply

SPINNING INSTRUCTIONS													
Wheel Ratio	3:1	3½:1	4:1	4½:1	5:1	5½:1	6:1	6½:1	7:1	8:1	9:1	10:1	12:1
'Feed in' in inches per treadle					½-¾	¾	¾	¾	1	1	1¼	1¼	1½
PLYING INSTRUCTIONS													
Per treadles per 18 inches					15	12	12	12	9	9	8	8	6

Armholes

K1, K2tog, at beg of next 12 rows. [108 sts]
Continue in patt until work measures 40 cm [15¾ in.].
Cast off.

SLEEVES

With 3 mm needles cast on 80 sts.
K1, P1 rib for 3 cm [1¼ in.].
Change to 3¾ mm needles and increase into every alternate st across row.   [120 sts]
Proceed in patt for 18 cm [7 in.].

Shape armholes

Next row K1, (K2tog) twice, work to last 5 sts, (K2tog) twice, K1.
Next row P1, (P2tog) twice, work to last 5 sts, (P2tog) twice, P1.
Repeat these last two rows twice.   [96 sts]
Continuing in patt, dec 1 st at each end of every row until 32 sts remain.
Work 1 row. Cast off.

YOKE

Using 3 mm needles cast on 40 sts.
1st row K.
2nd row P.
3rd row K16, turn, slip next st, purl to end.
4th row K32, turn, slip next st, purl to end.
Continue working these 4 rows until work measures 97 cm [38¼ in.] on *lower* edge of yoke.
Knit across all sts. Cast off.

TO MAKE UP

Measure centre of front of yoke.
Now from centre back measure 16½ cm [6½ in.] and place safety pin, then measure 14 cm [5½ in.] place safety pin, 36 cm [14½ in.] place safety pin, 14 cm [5½ in.] place safety pin leaving 16½ cm [6½ in.] to centre back.
Sew front half of jumper to 36 cm [14¼ in.] between 2nd and 3rd safety pins. One half of back to 16½ cm [6½ in.]; second half of back to 16½ cm [6½ in.]. Sleeves to be *eased* to each of the 14 cm [5½ in.] on each side. Sew side and sleeve seams.

NECK OPENING

Either with a small crochet hook double crochet down each side of neck opening, making 5 small buttonholes on the right-hand side, *or* with right side facing and using 3 mm needles pick up 32 sts evenly down side of neck edge. Knit 2 rows.
Buttonhole row K3, * yfwd, K2tog, K4, rep from * to last 3 sts, K3.
Knit 2 rows. Cast off.
Complete button side by using 3 mm needles and picking up 32 sts evenly. Knit 5 rows. Cast off.

NECK TRIMMING

With 3¾ mm needles and right side facing pick up 120 sts evenly around neck edge and work the 12 patt rows. Cast off.

TO MAKE UP

Fold neck trimming over so that the ribbon sits neatly on the front and couch down on right side.
Sew on buttons.

SKIRT BORDER

For hip measurements 87-92 cm [34-36 in.] cast on 330 sts.
For hip measurements 97-102 cm [38-40 in.] cast on 370 sts.
Using 3 mm needles cast on 330(370)sts and purl 4 rows.
Change to 3¾ mm needles and patt 4(5) complete patterns.
Change to 3 mm needles. Purl 4 rows. Cast off.
Sew border to lower edge of fabric skirt.

ANNABEL

Breed: Hebridean
Category: Shortwool and Down

It is the unique trimming on this slash neck sweater, knitted in dropped ladder stitch and completed with elasticated cuffs and waist, that turns a simple style into an up-to-date designer fashion.

MATERIALS

Handspun – Hebridean
11 threads per cm – single ply
27 threads per in. – single ply

Commercial equivalent – 4-ply
6.5 threads per cm
16 threads per in.

Handspun yarn
Note the Hebridean fleece has two shades, both of which were used.
Jacob fleece would be just as suitable.
300(350) g cream wool
100(100) g contrast

Commercial yarn
4(5) x 50 g balls of Schachenmayr Regia
3(3) x 50 g balls of Regia for the contrast

Approximately 1½ m [5 ft] of narrow elastic for waist and cuffs
Pair 3¾ mm (9) needles

MEASUREMENTS

To fit bust 81-87(92-97) cm [32-34(36-38) in.]
Length from top of shoulder 51(64) cm [20(25) in.]
Sleeve seam 42(45) cm [16½(17½) in.]

TENSION

28 sts and 36 rows to 10 cm [4 in.] measured over patt on 3¾ mm needles.

Special abbreviations
M1 – make one stitch by picking up horizontal loop lying before next stitch and working into back of it.
M – main; C – contrast

BACK AND FRONT (both alike)

With 3¾ mm needles and M cast on 67(77)sts and proceed as follows:
1st row With WS facing, K.
2nd row P.
3rd row (K10,M1) 6(7) times, K7.   [73(84)sts]
4th row P7 (K1,P10) 6(7) times.
5th row (K10,P1) 6(7) times, K7.
Repeat 4th and 5th rows twice more and 4th row once more.
Cast on 47(57)sts.   [120(141)sts]
Next row Set panel patt as follows:
K7, M1 (K10,M1) 4(5) times, K10, P1 to last 7 sts, K7.   [126(147)sts]
Change to C.
1st row P7, K1, * P10, K1, rep from * to last 7 sts, P7.
2nd row K7, P1, * K10, Pl, rep from * to last 7 sts, K7.
These 2 rows form panel patt. Cont in patt changing colour sequence as follows:
Work 25(30) more rows in C and then 27(36) rows M, 36(36) rows C, 27(36) rows C, 27(36) rows M, 27(32) rows C. Change to M.
Next row Cast off 47(57)sts loosely *as follows:* cast off the knit stitches, *drop the purl stitch off the needle,* (cast off 10 sts, drop the purl st off needle) 5 times, knit in patt to end.   [73(84)sts]
Work 8 rows in patt.

4-ply

SPINNING INSTRUCTIONS													
Wheel Ratio	3:1	3½:1	4:1	4½:1	5:1	5½:1	6:1	6½:1	7:1	8:1	9:1	10:1	12:1
'Feed in' in inches per treadle				¾	¾	1	1	1	1¼	1½	1½	1¾	2
PLYING INSTRUCTIONS													
Per treadles per 18 inches				12	12	9	9	9	8	6	6	5	4½

Next row K *at the same time* dropping all the purl stitches off the needle.
Next row P.
Cast off loosely.
With fingers gently run the dropped purl stitch to the beginning of work.

SLEEVES

Knitted in M throughout
With 3¾ mm needles cast on 104(110)sts.
1st row With WS facing, K.
2nd row P.
3rd row (K10,M1) 8(10) times, K10.
   [112(120)sts]
4th row (P10,K1) 8(10) times.
Rep 4th and 5th rows until work measures 45(47) cm [17½(18½) in.] ending with 4th row.
Cast off loosely *dropping all the purl stitches off the needle.*

TO MAKE UP

Press all pieces.
Join shoulder seams.
Set in sleeves carefully matching all ladder stitches on sleeves with the ladder stitch on back and front.

Sew up side and sleeve seams.
Turn back lower edge 1.5 cm [½ in.] and sew down, leaving gap in which to thread approximately 71 cm [28 in.] narrow elastic or according to comfortable waist measurements. Turn back and sew down 1.5 cm [½ in.] on each cuff and thread with elastic to comfortable wrist measurements (approximately 20 cm [8 in.]) firmly securing all elastic at seams.

COUCHING INSTRUCTIONS

For the commercial garment
Using oddments of double knitting yarn in suitable colours, prepare 10 strips of approximately 1 cm [½ in.] wide.
Place the strands in the *centre* of the knitted stripes and couch into place, securing all strands safely top and bottom.

For the handspun garment
Use the space dyed method yarn (see p. 64) and colour sequence as follows using Dylon cold water dye shades: A11 Tahiti Rose, A18 Nasturtium, A2 Sea Green, A30 Turquoise, A32 Bahama Blue and A3 Lilac.
Batt down and couch fibres 1 cm [½ in.] thick into place as above.

ANNABEL

KATHERINE

Fibres: Chinese Tussah silk noils
          Cotton

A very elegant two-piece day suit, suitable for all occasions, knitted in a beautiful lemon 100 per cent commercial cotton – hand or machine washable! – or handspun cotton and Chinese Tussah silk noils. The slubs in the Tussah silk noils give a similar texture to commercial cotton.

MATERIALS

Handspun
10 threads per cm – single ply
25 threads per in. – single ply

Commercial equivalent – double knitting (thin)
5.5 threads per cm
14 threads per in.

Handspun yarn
1000 g Chinese Tussah silk noils
1000 g cotton

Commercial yarn
29(30:32) x 50 g balls of Schachenmayr Micaela

Approx 1 m [3 ft] narrow elastic
18 buttons
2 beads
Pair each 3 mm (11) and 3¾ mm (9) needles

MEASUREMENTS

To fit bust 87(92:97) cm [34(36:38) in.]
Jacket: length 61(62:64) cm [24(24½:25) in.]
         sleeve seam 43(45:46) cm
              [17(17½:18) in.]

Skirt: To fit hips 107 cm [42 in.]
         length 69 cm [27 in.] adjustable

TENSION

Ridged rib stitch
25 sts and 32 rows to 10 cm [4 in.] measured over patt on 3¾ mm needles.

Rib stitch
30 sts and 30 rows to 10 cm [4 in.] measured over patt on 3 mm needles.

JACKET

BACK

* With 3 mm needles, cast on 72(75:78)sts and work in K1, P1 rib for 60(63:66) rows. *
Put work onto a spare needle.
Rep from * to *.
Place both pieces of work onto one needle. [144(150:156)sts]
Continue in rib until work measures 62(64:66) cm [24½(25½:26) in.] ending with wrong side.

Shape shoulders
Keeping patt correct, cast off 14 sts at beg of next 6 rows.
Cast off rem 60(66:72)sts.

FRONT

Left side
With 3¾ mm needles, cast on 57(59:61)sts and work in K1, P1 rib for 6 rows.
With RS facing commence in ridged rib patt as follows:
1st and 2nd rows K.
3rd row P1, * K1, P1, rep from * to end.
4th row K1, * P1, K1, rep from * to end.

DK (thin)

SPINNING INSTRUCTIONS												
Wheel Ratio	3:1	3½:1	4:1	4½:1	5:1	5½:1	6:1	6½:1	7:1	8:1	9:1	10:1	12:1
'Feed in' in inches per treadle		¾	¾	¾	1	1	1¼	1¼	1½	1½	1¾	2	2½
PLYING INSTRUCTIONS												
Per treadles per 18 inches		16	16	16	12	12	10	10	8	8	7	6	4½

KATHERINE

These 4 rows form patt.

Work in patt for 60(63:66) rows.

Next row K1, * yfwd, K2tog, rep from * to end.

Cont in patt until work measures 56(57:59) cm [22(22½:23) in.].

Shape neck

With WS facing cast off 7(9:11)sts at neck edge. Work to end of row.

Dec 1 st at end of next and every alt row for 16 rows ending with wrong side   [42 sts]

Shape shoulder

Keeping patt. correct, cast off 14 sts at beg of next row and every alt row until all sts are cast off.

RIGHT SIDE

Work as for left side, reversing all shapings.

SLEEVES

With 3¾ mm needles, cast on 63(65:67)sts and work in K1, P1 rib for 6 rows.

Change to ridged rib patt and inc 1st at each end of the next and every foll 4th row until work measures 43(45:46) cm [17(17½:18) in.). Cast off.

HALF BELT

With 3 mm needles, cast on 132(138:144)sts. Work 24 rows in K1, P1 rib. Cast off in rib.

TO MAKE UP

Collar and borders

Press lightly on wrong side with warm iron. Join shoulder seams.

Left front border

With 3¾ mm needles cast on 7 sts and work as follows:

1st row (RS) K1, * P1, K1, rep from * to end.

2nd row P1, * K1, P1, rep from * to end.

Rep these two rows until border fits up left front. (53.5 cm [21 in.])

Sew into position as you go along. Cast off neatly in rib.

Right front border

With 3¾ mm needles, cast on 7 sts and work in rib as for left front border for 22 cm [8¼ in.]. Make buttonhole as follows:

*1st row RS Rib 3, yfwd, K2tog, rib 2.

2nd row Rib.

3rd row As 1st row.

Rib 16 rows *.

Rep from * to * 3 times and then rows 1-3. Rib 2 rows.

With RS facing cast off in rib. Sew work into place as you go along.

COLLAR

With RS facing and using 3¾ mm needles, pick up 139(141:143)sts evenly around neck and K1, P1 rib for 7 rows. Cast off in rib.

Make two cords to thread through eyelet holes at waist, stitching ends of cords to side seams. Set in sleeves.

Join half belt to back of jacket, stitching each end into side seams.

Join side and sleeve seams.

Sew on buttons: two on each end of half belt, two on each sleeve cuff, ten on front band in five sets of two.

Bead ends of front cord, draw up and tie.

SKIRT

With 3 mm needles, cast on 330 sts and work in K1, P1 rib until work measures 69 cm [27 in.] or required length. Cast off in rib.

TO MAKE UP

Sew up seam.

Turn a casing of 2 cm [1 in.] and thread in elastic to fit waist. Press all seams.

OLWEN

Breed: Shetland
Category: Shortwool and Down
Other fibres: Cultivated silk
Mohair
Coloured worsted tops

Round neck sweater with long sleeves, knitted in a pretty eyelet pattern and threaded with ribbons.

MATERIALS

Handspun – Shetland, mohair and coloured worsted tops blended together
9 threads per cm – single ply
22 threads per in. – single ply

Handspun – silk
9 threads per cm – single ply
22 threads per in. – single ply

Commercial equivalent – double knitting (thick)
5 threads per cm
12 threads per in.

Handspun yarn
(1) 200 g white Shetland
150 g white mohair
50 g coloured worsted tops (lilac) } blended together
(2) 250 g cultivated silk
(1) and (2) are plyed together.

Commercial yarn
8 x 50 g balls of Scheepjeswol Ribbon Mohair

Approx 0.6 cm [¼ in.] wide single faced satin ribbon:
5 metres [15 feet] light lilac
5 metres [15 feet] medium lilac
4 metres [12 feet] dark lilac
Pair each of 4½ mm (7) and 5½ mm (5) needles

MEASUREMENTS

To fit bust 86-91.5 cm [34-36 in.]
Length from top of shoulder 54 cm [21¼ in.]
Sleeve seam 50 cm [19½ in.]

TENSION

16 sts and 20 rows to 10 cm [4 in.] measured over patt on 5½ mm needles.

BACK

** With 5½ mm needles cast on 67 sts and work in patt as follows:
1st and 2nd rows K.
3rd row K2 * yfwd, K2tog, rep from * to last st, K1.
4th and 5th rows K.
6th, 8th, 10th and 12th rows P.
7th row K3, (yfwd, Sl1, K1, psso, K6) 8 times.
9th row K1, * K2tog, yfwd, K1, yfwd, Sl1, K1, psso, K3, rep from * to last 2 sts, K2.
11th row As 7th row.
13th-18th rows As rows 1-6.
19th row K7, * yfwd, Sl1, K1, psso, K6, rep from * to last 4 sts, yfwd, Sl1, K1, psso, K2.
20th and 22nd row P.
21st row K5, * K2tog, yfwd, K1, yfwd, Sl1, K1, psso, K3, rep from * to last 6 sts, K2tog, yfwd, K1, yfwd, Sl1, K1, psso, K1.
23rd row As 19th row.
24th row P.
These 24 rows form patt.
Repeat patt rows 1-6.**

DK (thick)

SPINNING INSTRUCTIONS													
Wheel Ratio	3:1	3½:1	4:1	4½:1	5:1	5½:1	6:1	6½:1	7:1	8:1	9:1	10:1	12:1
'Feed in' in inches per treadle	½-¾	½-¾	½-¾	1	1	1¼	1¼	1½	1½	1¾	2	2¼	2½
PLYING INSTRUCTIONS													
Per treadles per 18 inches	19	19	19	12	12	10	10	8	8	7	6	5	4½

Shape neck as follows keeping patt straight:
7th row Cast off 3 sts, patt to end.
Work 2 rows dec 1 st at neck edge on each row.
Work on these sts until 21st row is reached on the *second* complete patt from neck shaping.
21st and 22nd rows Inc 1 st at neck edge only.
23rd row Cast on 3 sts, patt to end.
24th row P.
Rep patt rows 1-24 and then patt rows 1-6.
Cast off loosely.

FRONT

Work as for back from ** to **.

Shape neck as follows keeping patt straight:
7th row Cast off 4 sts, patt to end.
Work two rows dec 1 st at neck edge on each row.
Work on these sts until 21st row is reached on the *second* complete patt from neck shaping.
21st and 22nd rows Inc 1 st at neck edge only.
23rd row Cast on 4 sts, patt to end.
24th row P.
Rep patt rows 1-24 and then rows 1-6.
Cast off loosely.

SLEEVES (both alike)

Using 4½ mm needles, cast on 33 sts and work 8 cm [3½ in.] in K1, P1 rib.
Change to 5½ mm needles.
Next row Inc 20 sts evenly across row.   [53 sts]
Next row P.
Proceed in patt as follows:
1st and 2nd rows K.
3rd row K2, * yfwd, K2tog, rep from * to last st, K1.

4th and 5th rows K.
6th, 8th, 10th and 12th rows P.
7th row K3, (yfwd, Sl1, K1, psso, K6) 6 times, K2.
9th row K1, * K2tog, yfwd, K1, yfwd, Sl1, K1, psso, K3, rep from * to last 4 sts, K4.
11th row As 7th row.
13th-18th rows As rows 1-6.
19th row K7, * yfwd, Sl1, K1, psso, K6, rep from * to last 6 sts, yfwd, Sl1, K1, psso, K4.
20th and 22nd rows P.
21st row K5, * K2tog, yfwd, K1, yfwd, Sl1, K1, psso, K3, rep from * to end.
23rd row As 19th row.
24th row P.
These 24 rows form patt.
Rep these patt rows three times more.
Next row K.
Next row P.
Cast off loosely.

MAKE UP AND NECK BORDER

Join right shoulder seam.

Neck border
With RS facing and 4½ mm needles pick up and knit 36 sts evenly across back and 40 sts evenly across front.   [76 sts]
Work in K1, P1 rib for 5 cm [2 in.]. Cast off loosely in rib.
Join left shoulder and neck border.
Place centre of sleeve to shoulder seam, sew in sleeves.
Join side and sleeve seams.
Press lightly on wrong side.
Thread ribbons through eyelet holes and secure on WS of work.

OLWEN

MARGARET

Category: Cultivated silk
Other fibre: Silk

Stunning lacy sweater in luxurious fibre with the panels edged with picot trim and a white pearl bead sewn to each picot peak.

MATERIALS

Handspun – silk
8 threads per cm – single ply
20 threads per in. – single ply

Commercial equivalent – Aran (thin)
4.5 threads per cm
11 threads per in.

Handspun yarn
350(375:400) g cultivated silk
4 pots Dylon cold water dye shade A50 Charcoal
(*Note* to obtain black always double the amount of charcoal dye required.)

Commercial yarn
9(10:11) x 50 g balls of Jaeger Luxury Spun Wool/Alpaca

Pair each 3¼ mm (10) and 4 mm (8) needles
Approx 300 pearl beads

MEASUREMENTS

To fit bust 91(97:102) cm [36(38:40) in.]
Length 61(62:63) cm [24(24½:25) in.]
Sleeve seam 41 cm [16 in.]

TENSION

22 sts and 30 rows to 10 cm [4 in.] on 4 mm needles.

Special abbreviations

Tw2f – twist 2 front (knit into front of second stitch on left hand needle then into front of first stitch and slip both stitches off needle together).
Tw2b – twist 2 back (knit into back of second stitch on left hand needle then into back of first stitch and slip both stitches off needle together).

FRONT AND BACK PANEL PATTERN (40 sts)

1st row P3, * Tw2f, Tw2b, K1, K2tog, yf, K1, yf, Sl1, K1, psso, K1, Tw2f, Tw2b *, P4 rep from * to *, P3.
2nd and foll alt rows K3, P15, K4, P15, K3.
3rd row P3, * Tw2b, Tw2f, K2tog, yf, K3, yf, Sl1, K1, psso, Tw2b, Tw2f *, P4, rep from * to *, P3.
5th row P3, * Tw2f, Tw2b, K1, yf, Sl1, psso, K1, K2tog, yf, K1, Tw2f, Tw2b *, P4, rep from * to *, P3.
7th row P3 * Tw2b, Tw2f, K2, yf, Sl1, K2tog, psso, yf, K2, Tw2b, Tw2f *, P4, rep from * to *, P3.
8th row As 2nd.
These eight rows form pattern.

SLEEVE PANEL PATTERN (21 sts)

1st row P3, Tw2f, Tw2b, K1, K2tog, yf, K1, yf, Sl1, K1, psso, K1, Tw2f, Tw2b, P3.
2nd and foll alt rows K3, P to last 3 sts, K3.
3rd row P3, Tw2b, Tw2f, K2tog, yf, K3, yf, Sl1, K1, psso, Tw2b, Tw2f, P3.
5th row P3, Tw2f, Tw2b, K1, yf, Sl1, K1, psso, K1, K2tog, yf, K1, Tw2f, Tw2b, P3.
7th row P3, Tw2b, Tw2f, K2, yf, Sl1, K2tog, psso, yf, K2, Tw2b, Tw2f, P3.
8th row As 2nd.
These eight rows form pattern.

Aran (thin)

SPINNING INSTRUCTIONS													
Wheel Ratio	3:1	3½:1	4:1	4½:1	5:1	5½:1	6:1	6½:1	7:1	8:1	9:1	10:1	12:1
'Feed in' in inches per treadle	½-¾	¾	¾	¾	1	1	1¼	1¼	1½	1¾	2	2¼	2½
PLYING INSTRUCTIONS													
Per treadles per 18 inches	19	16	16	16	12	12	10	10	8	7	6	5	4½

MARGARET

BACK

With 3¼ mm needles, cast on 96(102:108)sts and work in K1, P1 rib for 6 cm [2½ in.].
Next row Rib 5(8:11)sts, (inc in next st, rib 4) 17 times, inc into next st, rib 5(8:11). [114(120:126)sts]
Change to 4 mm needles and continue in patt as follows:
1st row (RS), P18(21:23) * (K3, P5) twice, K3 *, panel patt 1st row, rep from * to *, P18(21:23).
2nd row K18(21:23), * (P3, K5) twice, P3 *, panel patt 2nd row, rep from * to *, K18(21:23).
These 2 rows form patt. Continue with these two rows but working the 8 row panel patt until work measures 41 cm [16 in.].

Shape armholes

Cast off 3 sts at beg of next 6 rows. Dec 1 st at *both* ends of every row until 82(86:90)sts are left. **
Cont straight until armholes measure 20(21:22) cm [8(8¼:8¾) in.].

Shape shoulders

Cast off 12 sts at beg of next 2 rows and 12(13:14)sts at beg of foll two rows. Leave rem 34(36:38)sts on safety pin.

FRONT

Work as for back to **.
Cont straight until armholes measure 12(13:14) cm [4¾(5:5½) in.] ending WS.

Shape neck

Patt 31(33:34), turn and cont on these sts. Dec 1 st at neck edge on next and foll alt rows until 24 sts are left.
Cont straight until armholes match back to shoulder, ending at armhole edge.

Shape shoulders

Cast off 12 sts at beg of next row. Work 1 row. Cast off rem sts.
With RS facing slip centre 16(18:20)sts onto safety pin. Rejoin yarn to rem sts and work to match first side reversing shaping.

SLEEVES

With 3¼ mm needles cast on 42(46:50)sts and

K1, P1 rib for 5 cm [2 in.].
Next row Rib 3(5:7), (inc into next st) 35 times, rib 4(6:8) [77(81:85)sts].
Change to 4 mm needles and with RS facing P17(19:23), K3, P5, K3, panel patt 1st row, K3, P5, K3, P17(19:23).
Next row K17(19:23), P3, K5, P3, panel patt 2nd row, P3, K5, P3, K17(19:23).
These 2 rows form patt. Keeping panel patt correct continue straight until work measures 41 cm [16 in.] ending with a 2nd row.

Shape top

With RS facing, cast off 3 sts at beg of next 6 rows. Dec 1 st at both ends of next and every foll alt row until 32 sts remain, then both ends of every row until 22 sts remain.
Cast off 3 sts at beg of next 4 rows. Cast of rem sts.

NECK BAND

Join right shoulder.
With 3¼ mm needles pick up and K24 sts down left front neck, K centre front sts, inc 4 sts evenly. Pick up and K24 sts up right front neck. Knit centre back sts. [102(106:110)sts]
K1, P1, rib for 5 cm [2 in.].
Cast off to form picot edge as follows: cast off 2 sts, *slip st back onto left hand needle, cast on 2 sts, cast off 4 sts, rep from * to end.

TO MAKE UP

Join left shoulder and neckband seam.
Sew side and sleeve seams.
Set in sleeves.

TO DECORATE

Using 3¼ mm needles pick up and knit 150 sts evenly alongside first K3 sts on edge of both sides of panel patt. Cast off picot edge.
Pick up and knit 120 sts along both sides of sleeve panel.
Cast off picot edge.
Sew a pearl bead to each picot tip on sides of panels and neck.

EUNICE

Breed: Romney
Category: Longwool and Lustre

Remember that first textured yarn – here is a simple sweater to make with those first attempts. Back, front and sleeves are all knitted from the top down so when it is long enough for you, simply cast off.

MATERIALS

Handspun – Romney
5.5 threads per cm – single ply
13 threads per in. – single ply

Commercial equivalent – chunky
3 threads per cm
7/8 threads per in.

Handspun yarn
approx 550(600) g Romney

Commercial yarn
7(8) x 100 g balls of Twilleys soft 2-ply cotton

5 m [15 ft] ribbon
Beads of choice
Pair each 4½ mm (7) and 10 mm (000) needles

MEASUREMENTS

To fit bust 81–86(91-97) cm [32-34(36-38) in.]
Length from top of shoulders 44-47 cm [17¼-18½ in.]
Sleeve seam 41-47 cm [16-18½ in.]

TENSION

10 sts and 15 rows to 10 cm [4 in.] measured over garter stitch (every row knit) on 10 mm needles.

BACK AND FRONT (both alike)

With 10 mm needles, cast on 46(50)sts. Knit 50(56) rows. (34-38 cm) [13¼-15 in.] or desired length.
Change to 4½ mm needles and K1, P1 rib for 12 rows (9 cm [3½ in.]).
Cast off.

SLEEVES

With 10 mm needles cast on 40 sts *loosely*. Knit 46(56) rows, (32-38 cm) [12½-15 in.] or desired length.
Change to 4½ mm needles and K1, P1 rib for 12 rows (9 cm [3½ in.]).
Cast off.

TO MAKE UP

Leaving gap of 22 cm [8½ in.] for head, join shoulders.
Placing centre of sleeves to shoulder seam, sew in sleeves.
Join side and sleeve seams.
Weave in ribbon where required, such as across neck, down front, around sleeves, and sew on beads to complete decoration. (See photo overleaf.)

Chunky

SPINNING INSTRUCTIONS													
Wheel Ratio	3:1	3½:1	4:1	4½:1	5:1	5½:1	6:1	6½:1	7:1	8:1	9:1	10:1	12:1
'Feed in' in inches per treadle	1¼	1½	1½	1¾	2	2	2½	2½	3	3	3½	4	4
PLYING INSTRUCTIONS													
Per treadles per 18 inches	10	8	8	7	6	6	4½	4½	4	4	3	3	3

EUNICE

·3·

Icelandic

With Icelandic or Lopi yarn ignore all previous spinning instructions to ply the yarn. Icelandic is a single ply! But it must be spun at exactly 21 degrees.

In fact quite a few commercial fashion mohair yarns are single spun, and as long as the degree is maintained then the yarn will not disintegrate or garments spiral when knitted. No variation must be made to the spinning instructions. The degree is maintained by these instructions. It is therefore important that the fibres are well prepared.

Drum carding is a great help in this preparation as are commercially combed worsted tops. However, whether using rolags, drum carded or worsted tops, break down the fibres into strips or batts (as in fig. 8) and then pull the rolag, strips or batts into a roving (see fig. 9) as near to the thickness of 3.5 threads per centimetre [9 threads per in.] as possible,

checking the thickness by slightly twisting and winding the fibres around a rod or pencil, measuring the threads in cm or in. as you go (see fig. 10). The feed in is quite fast, and consequently there will be no time to pull out the fibres to the required thickness whilst you are spinning. You will only have time to gently feed them into the orifice.

Whatever the feed in instructions, do it – it will not fall apart! It really does work and you will end up with quick and exciting Icelandic yarn that is not only fast to spin but quick and easy to knit. A very helpful asset is a large plastic bucket! Pull out all the fibres to the thickness required letting them fall softly and continuously into the bucket. This way masses of yarn can be prepared ready to just feed onto the spinning wheel. Bearing in mind that most Icelandic sweaters need upwards of 500 g yarn, the spinning takes hardly any time at all.

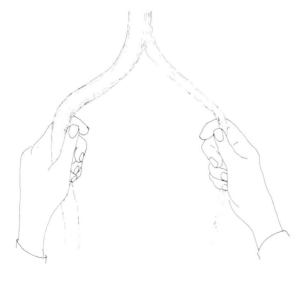

8   *Break fibres into strips*

9   *Pull into rovings as near to correct thickness as possible*

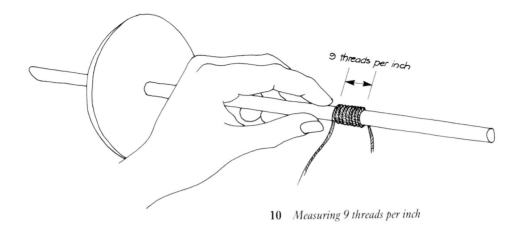

10 *Measuring 9 threads per inch*

NORMAN

Breed: Swaledale
Category: Mountain and Hill

There will always be a variation in thickness or evenness of the spinning of Lopi yarn, either commercial or handspun, so the ideal stitch to work with is the fisherman's rib. Try this classic styled sweater loved by all. It has been designed to fit very loosely so pass it around for the family to wear, from your man to teenage son or daughter!

MATERIALS

Handspun – Swaledale
3.5 threads per cm – single ply
9 threads per in. – single ply

Commercial equivalent – Icelandic or Lopi yarn
This is a single ply yarn
3.5 threads per cm – single ply
9 threads per in. – single ply

Handspun yarn
1000(1100:1200) g Swaledale

Commercial yarn
10(11:12) x 100 g balls of Samband Lopi

Pair each 5 mm (6) and 6 mm (4) needles

MEASUREMENTS

To fit bust/chest 87(90:97) cm [34(36:38) in.]
Actual measurements 107(114:121) cm [42(45:48) in.]
Length from centre back (excluding collar) 68(70:72) cm [26½(27½:28½) in.]
Sleeve seam 46(47:48) cm [18(18½:19) in.]

TENSION

11 sts and 20 rows to 10 cm [4 in.] on 6 mm needles over patt.

Special abbreviations

K1B – K1 below by K next st but in the row *below*, inserting needle through work and allowing st above to drop off needle.

Lopi

SPINNING INSTRUCTIONS													
Wheel Ratio	3:1	3½:1	4:1	4½:1	5:1	5½:1	6:1	6½:1	7:1	8:1	9:1	10:1	12:1
'Feed in' in inches per treadle	1½	1¾	2	2¼	2½	2½	3	3	3½	4	4½		
PLYING INSTRUCTIONS					There are no plying instructions – this is a single ply yarn								

NORMAN

BACK

** With 5 mm needles cast on 59(63:67)sts and work in rib as follows:

1st row (RS) K1, * P1, K1, rep from * to end.
2nd row P1, * K1, P1, rep from * to end.

Rep these 2 rows until work measures 7 cm [3 in.], ending with RS facing.

Change to 6 mm needles and work in patt as follows:

1st row K.
2nd row K1, * K1B, P1, rep from * to last 2 sts, K1B, K1.

These 2 rows form patt and are repeated throughout.

Work straight in patt until back measures 40(41:42) cm [15¾(16:16½) in.] ending with second patt row. Place marker at each end of this row to indicate beginning of armhole shaping.

Shape raglan armholes

Work 4 rows in patt.
5th row (RS) K4, K3tog, K to last 7 sts, K3tog tbl, K4.
6th row As 2nd patt row.

Rep last 6 rows 4(3:2) times more, then cont shaping as follows:

Work 2 rows straight, then rep 5th and 6th rows. **

Rep these last 4 rows 4(6:8) times more.
Cast off rem 19 sts *loosely*.

FRONT

Work as for back from ** to **.
Rep last 4 rows 2(3:4) times more.
Work 2 rows straight ending with 2nd patt row. [27 sts]

Shape front neck
1st row (RS) K4, K3tog, K3 and leave these sts on a stitch holder for left front. Cast off next 7 sts, K to last 7 sts, K3tog tbl, K4.
Cont on rem 8 sts for right front.

2nd row Work without shaping.
3rd row Cast off 2 sts, K to end.
4th row As 2nd row.
5th row K2tog tbl, K4.
6th row K1, K1B, P1, P2tog.
Cast off rem 4 sts.
Rejoin yarn to neck edge of left front sts.
Cast off 2 sts, patt to end.
Work 2 rows straight.
Next row K4, K2tog.
Next row P2tog, P1, K1B, K1.
Cast off rem 4 sts.

SLEEVES

With 5 mm needles cast on 35(39:43)sts and work in rib as given for back for 6 cm [2½ in.] ending with RS facing.

Change to 6 mm needles and work in patt as given for back, inc 1 st at both ends of every foll 10th row 6 times (working incs into patt). [47(51:55)sts]

Cont without shaping until sleeve measures 46(47:48) cm [18(18½:19) in.] ending with 2nd patt row.

Shape raglan top
Work as for back raglan until 11 sts remain.
Rep 1st and 2nd patt rows.
Next row K4, K3tog, K4.
Next row K1, K1B, P1, P3tog, P1, K1B, K1.
Cast off rem 7 sts.

COLLAR

With 5 mm needles cast on 71 sts and work in rib as given for back welt until collar measures 18 cm [7 in.] ending with 2nd rib row.
Cast off in rib.

TO MAKE UP

Join raglan, side and sleeve seams. Sew side seam of collar and slip stitch to neck. Fold collar over onto right side.

BELLE

Breed: Cheviot
Category: Mountain and Hill

Belle, meaning lovely, is just what this two-tone fisherman's rib lady's cardigan is – casual yet smart, comfortable yet fashionable. It is simply knitted on a circular needle.

One always associates the circular needle with yoke-knitted sweaters or working in rounds. However, the advantages of working backwards and forwards with a circular needle are fourfold:
1. No long needles to catch on sides of armchairs or indeed people sitting next to you on buses or trains!
2. No weight on wrists. The weight of your work is in your lap.
3. Stitches can rest when not being worked on the wires between the ends and will not be stretched.
4. Probably the best reason – never to lose the other needle for it is always on the end of your work!

Spinning and plying instructions as for *Norman* (p. 38).

MATERIALS

Handspun – Cheviot
3.5 threads per cm – single ply
9 threads per in. – single ply

Commercial equivalent – Icelandic or Lopi yarn
This is a single ply yarn
3.5 threads per cm – single ply
9 threads per in. – single ply

Handspun yarn
600(700:800:800) g main
400(500:600:600) g contrast

Commercial yarn
7(8:9:9) x 100 g balls of Samband Lopi in main shade
5(6:7:7) x 100 g balls Samband Lopi in contrast

Pair each 5 mm (6) needles
6 mm (4) circular needle 100 cm long
Cable needle
9 buttons

MEASUREMENTS

To fit bust 87(90:97:102) cm [34(36:38:40) in.]
Actual measurements 99(104:112:117) cm [39(41:44:46) in.]
Length at centre back excluding neck band 61 cm [24 in.]
Sleeve seam 45 cm [17½ in.]

TENSION

14 sts and 32 rows to 10 cm [4 in.] on 6 mm needles over patt.

Special abbreviations

M – main colour; C – contrast; C4f – cable 4 sts forward by slipping next 4 sts onto a cable needle and holding at front of work, work in pattern over next 4 sts then work over the 4 sts from the cable needle.

The two row repeat of the standard fisherman's rib pattern becomes a four row repeat in this version, each colour being used alternately, once working into the stitch below the purl stitch and once working into the stitch below the knit stitch. The secret lies in which side the work is facing for each row and for this it is necessary to work on a circular needle so that the work can be pushed back to the needle tip *without* turning the work around.

In trying to remember which row you are on:
1. The colours will alternate, so if the main colour is on the needle then you will use the contrast colour next, and vice versa.
2. The yarn to be used next is always picked up at the edge where it is hanging, so if you do forget whether or not to turn, the position of the colour you are to use next will automatically let you know because you start with the colour from the right edge.

To remember whether to work into the stitch below (or double stitch) with a knit or purl is a little more difficult:
1. You must never work into a double stitch made on the previous row.
2. Should you make a mistake the colours will show up wrong, i.e. contrast will appear on main and vice versa.

BACK

With 5 mm needles and M, cast on

BELLE

79(83:89:93)sts and work in K1, P1 rib for 5 cm [2 in.] ending with a WS row.

Still in M, change to 6 mm circular needle and work preparation row.

Preparation row K1, * P1, K1, rep from * to end. *Do not turn.* Push sts back to right needle tip.

Now proceed in patt as follows:

1st row With RS facing and C, K1, * P into st below next st on left needle, K1, rep from * to end, *turn.*

2nd row With WS facing and M, K1, K into st below next st on left needle, rep from * to last 2 sts, K2. *Do not turn* but push sts back to right needle tip.

3rd row With WS facing and C, P1, * K into st below next st on left needle, P1, rep from * to end, *turn.*

4th row With RS facing and M, K1, * P1, K into st below next st on left needle, rep from * to last 2 sts, P1, K1. *Do not turn*, but push sts back to right needle tip.

These 4 rows from patt. Cont straight in patt until work measures 41 cm [16 in.] from cast on edge ending with WS and first row of patt.

Shape raglan armholes

Keeping patt correct, cast off 4(4:6:6)sts at beg of next 2 rows.

Next row Sl1, K2tog, psso, work to last 3 sts, Sl1, K2tog, psso.

Work 2 rows.

Repeat dec row.

Now continue to dec 4 sts on every 4th row until 27 sts remain.

Work 3 rows. Cast off.

POCKET LINING (make two)

With 5 mm needles cast on 23 sts and work in st st for 10 cm [4 in.] ending with WS.

Leave sts on a spare needle.

LEFT FRONT

Using 5 mm needles and M cast on 45(47:51:53)sts.

Work in K1, P1 rib for 5 cm [2 in.] ending with WS.

Still in M, change to 6 mm circular needle and work preparation row as given for back.

Now proceed in patt as follows:

1st row RS facing and C, K1, * P into st below next st on left needle, K1, rep from * to end, *turn.*

2nd row With WS facing and M, K1, K into st below next st on left needle, rep from * to last 2 sts, K2. *Do not turn* but push sts back to right needle tip.

3rd row WS facing and C, P1, * K into st below next st on left needle, P1, rep from * to end. *Turn.*

4th row RS facing and M, K1, * P1, K into st below next st on left needle, rep from * to last 2 sts, P1, K1. *Do not turn*, but push sts back to right needle tip.

These 4 rows form patt. Continue in patt keeping colours correct until work measures 10 cm [4 in.] from top of welt, ending with 3rd row of patt.

Place pocket

Next row K6(8:12:14)sts, slip next 23 sts onto a stitch holder, and in their place K across sts of one pocket lining, patt to end of row. [45(47:51:53)sts]

Work 16 patt rows.

Work cable patt as follows:

Work 14(16:20:22)sts, slip next 4 sts onto a cable needle and leave at front of work, patt 4 sts, then patt 4 sts from cable needle, patt to end.

Continue working in patt until work measures 41 cm [16 in.] ending at armhole edge *at the same time* on row one of every four complete patterns (16 rows) work the cable row.

Shape armhole

Keeping patt correct, cast off 4(4:6:6)sts at beg of next row.

Next row Patt to last 3 sts, P3.

Next row Sl1, K3tog, psso, patt to end.

Continue to dec 3 sts at armhole edge every 4th row until 20 sts remain. Work 1 row.

Shape front neck

Cast off 2 sts at neck edge, patt to end.

Rejoin yarn and work one row.

Cont to dec 3 sts at armhole edge *as before* and on the same 4th row dec 1 st at neck edge until 2 sts remain.

Work 3 rows. Cast off. [48 rows]

RIGHT FRONT

Using 5 mm needles and M, cast on 45(47:51:53)sts and work in K1, P1 rib for 5 cm [2 in.] ending with WS.

Still in M change to 6 mm circular needle and work as for left front reversing all shapings and placing pocket as follows:

Next row RS facing, K8, slip next 23 sts onto a stitch holder and in their place K across sts of 2nd pocket lining, K to end.

SLEEVES

Using 5 mm needles and M, cast on 41(43:45:47)sts and work in K1, P1 rib for 8 cm [3 in.].

Still in M, change to 6 mm circular needle and starting with preparation row work in patt as given for back, inc 1 st at each end of 3rd and every foll 4th row until there are 63(67:71:75)sts on the needle, working inc sts into patt.

Cont straight in patt until work measures 45 cm [17½ in.] from cast on edge, ending with WS.

Shape raglan top

Keeping patt correct, cast off 4(4:6:6)sts at beg of next 2 rows.

Next row Sl1, K2tog, psso, work to last 3 sts, Sl1, K2tog, psso.

Work 2 rows.

Rep dec row.

Now cont to dec 4 sts on every 4th row as for back until 11 sts remain. Work 3 rows. Cast off.

LEFT FRONT BORDER

With 5 mm needles and M, cast on 8 sts and work in K1, P1 rib for front border, slightly stretching and sewing border into place as it is being worked.

Mark all button positions on this border as follows:

The top button will be on the 2nd and 3rd rows of neckband and the bottom button will be on the 5th and 6th row of rib and the remaining 7 buttons spaced evenly between.

RIGHT FRONT BORDER

Work as for left front border but work buttonholes as placed on the left as follows:
With RS facing, rib 3, cast off 2 sts, rib to end.
Next row Rib 3, cast on 2 sts, rib to end.

NECK BAND

Join all raglan seams. With RS facing and 5 mm needles rib across 8 sts of right front border, K up 21 sts from right slope, 11 sts from right sleeve top, 27 sts across back of neck, 11 sts from left sleeve top, 21 sts from left slope and rib across 8 sts from left front border. [107 sts] Work 7 rows in K1, P1 rib, working a button-hole, as before, on 2nd and 3rd row. Cast off in rib.

POCKET TOPS (both alike)

With RS facing and 6 mm needles work across the 23 sts of one pocket top, increasing 1 st at each end of this row only. Work 5 more rows in rib. Cast off in rib.

TO MAKE UP

Neatly stitch pocket linings and tops into place.
Join side and sleeve seams.
Add buttons to correspond with buttonholes.

Thick and thin spiral

This is a very easy and straightforward yarn to create, made by spinning a thin double knitting thread and a chunky thread and allowing one to wrap the other. It is a very popular fashion yarn for most commercial spinners.

Colour and almost any yarn you choose to use will make the combinations of this yarn endless. In the following two designs I have only added a fine silver thread, to 'hold' with the thin double knitting yarn, to soften as in the case of the pure white sweater and to startle in the grey and black design.

PHOEBE

Breed: Romney
Category: Longwool and Lustre

Snowy white with a hint of silver glitter makes this bobble textured sweater, with its pretty puffed three-quarter length sleeves, a must for every wardrobe.

MATERIALS

Handspun – Romney double knitting (thin)
10 threads per cm – single ply
25 threads per in. – single ply

Handspun – Romney chunky
5.5 threads per cm – single ply
13 threads per in. – single ply

Commercial equivalent – double-double
3.5 threads per cm
9 threads per in.

Handspun yarn
550(550:650) g Romney

Optional
Fine silver thread to ply with double knitting thin yarn

Commercial yarn
6(6:7) x 100 g balls of Emu Mikado

Pair each 6 mm (4) and 7 mm (2) needles

MEASUREMENTS

To fit bust 81(86:91) cm [32(34:36) in.]
Length 59(60:61) cm [23(23½:24) in.]
Sleeve seam (three-quarter length) approx 28 cm [11 in.]

TENSION

12 sts and 18 rows to 10 cm [4 in.] on 7 mm needles.

Special abbreviation
Make bobble – knit into the front and back of the next st until you have made 5 sts, turn, P5 sts, turn, K5 sts, then slip 5th, 4th, 3rd and 2nd sts over 1st st.

BACK AND FRONT (both alike)

With 6 mm needles cast on 40(42:46)sts and work in K1, P1 rib for 8 cm [3 in.] inc 7 sts evenly across last row.   [47(49:53)sts]
Change to 7 mm needles and work 10 rows in st st.
11th row K, inc 1 st at each end of the row. [49(51:55)sts]

Work 5 more rows in st st.

17th row * K6, make bobble, rep from * to last 7(9:4)sts, K7(9:4).

18th row P.

Work rows 1-18 incl twice more, working inc sts into bobble row. [53(55:59)sts]

Cont to make bobble on every 17th row.

Work straight until work measures 35.5 cm [14 in.]

Shape armholes

Cast off 3 sts at beg of next 2 rows. [47(49:53)sts]

Next row K2tog, work to last 2 sts, K2tog.

Work 1 row.

Rep last 2 rows once more. [43(45:49)sts]

Cont straight until work measures 59(60:61) cm [23(23½:24) in.]

Shape shoulders

Cast off 10(10:12)sts, slip next 23(25:29)sts onto a spare needle, cast off rem 10(10:12)sts.

SLEEVES

Using 6 mm needles, cast on 31(31:33)sts and work in K1, P1 rib for 8 cm [3 in.] inc 4 sts evenly across last row. [35(35:37)sts]

Change to 7 mm needles and continue to work the 18 rows as for back, inc 1 st each end of every 11th row and making bobble on every

17th row until there are 39(39:41)sts.

Cont working straight until work measures 28 cm [11 in.] ending WS.

Shape top

Cast off 3 sts at beg of next 2 rows. [33(33:35)sts]

Next row K2tog, K to last 2 sts, K2tog.

Work 1 row.

Rep last 2 rows once more. [29(29:31)sts]

Cont straight on these sts until work measures 19(20.5:21.5) cm [7½(8:8½) in.] ending WS.

Next row K2tog across row.

Next row P2tog across row.

Cast off rem sts.

NECK BAND (back)

Slip 23(25:29)sts from back of neck onto 6 mm needles. Rejoin yarn and K2tog, then K1, P1 rib across row to last 2 sts, K2tog.

Work 3 more rows in rib. Cast off.

NECK BAND (front)

Repeat as for back.

TO MAKE UP

Sew neck and shoulder seams.

Set in sleeves.

Sew side and sleeve seams.

Thick and thin spiral

SPINNING INSTRUCTIONS													
Wheel Ratio	3:1	3½:1	4:1	4½:1	5:1	5½:1	6:1	6½:1	7:1	8:1	9:1	10:1	12:1
'Feed in' in inches per treadle													
DK (thin)			½	½	¾	¾	¾	1	1	1¼	1¼	1½	1¾
Chunky	1½	1½	1½	1¾	2	2	2½	2½	3	3	3½	4	4
PLYING INSTRUCTIONS	Work near to the orifice with both hands. Hold the thin strand in the left hand and the chunky strand in the right hand. Feed both yarns evenly into the orifice allowing the chunky strand to 'wrap' the thin strand.												

PHOEBE

ERICA

Breed: Romney
Category: Longwool and Lustre

Classic V-neck raglan sleeve sweater with detachable collar/hood. Ideal for those sunny autumn walks. (See page 46 for spinning and plying chart.)

MATERIALS

Handspun – Romney double knitting (thin)
10 threads per cm – single ply
25 threads per in. – single ply

Handspun – Romney chunky
5.5 threads per cm – single ply
13 threads per in. – single ply

Commercial equivalent – double-double
3.5 threads per cm
9 threads per in.

Handspun yarn
Sweater
300(400:550) g Romney
Hood
200(200:200) g Romney
4(5:5) pots Dylon cold water dye shade A50 Charcoal
(*Note* to obtain black always double the amount of charcoal dye required.)

Optional
Fine silver thread to ply with double knitting thin yarn

Commercial yarn
Sweater
4(4:5) x 100 g balls of Emu Mikado
Hood
2(2:2) x 100 g balls of Emu Mikado

7 buttons for hood.
Pair each 6 mm (4) and 7 mm (2) needles

MEASUREMENTS

To fit bust 86(91:97:102) cm [34(36:38:40) in.]
Length 60(60:61:61) cm [23½(23½:24:24) in.]
Sleeve seam 44 cm [17½ in.]

TENSION

12 sts and 18 rows to 10 cm [4 in.] on 7 mm needles.

BACK

With 6 mm needles cast on 57(61:63:67)sts and work in K1, P1 rib for 6 cm [2½ in.].
Change to 7 mm needles and work in st st until work measures 38 cm [15 in.] ending WS.

Shape armholes
Cast off 3 sts at beg of next 2 rows. **
Dec 1 st at each end of next and every alternate row until 17(25:24:33)sts remain.
Work 2(6:6:10) rows dec 1 st at each end of every row.   [13 sts]
Leave these sts on a spare needle.

FRONT

Work as for Back until **.
Divide for neck
K2tog, K23(25:26:28), turn. Work on these sts as follows.
Next row K1, purl to last st, K1.
Cont working in st st, dec 1 st at armhole edge on the next row and every alt row *at the same time* dec 1 st at neck edge on the next row and every other 6th row until there are 6(8:9:11)sts.
Work a further 6(2:4:0) rows, dec at armhole edge only in next and every alt row. [3(7:7:11)sts]
Work 0(4:4:8) rows dec only at armhole edge on every row.   [3 sts]
Next row K2tog, K1.
Next row K2tog.
With RS facing slip 1 st of rem 26(28:29:31)sts onto a safety pin. Rejoin yarn and knit to last 2 sts, K2tog.
Next row K1, purl to last st, K1.
Now work as given for left front, reversing all shapings.

SLEEVES

Using 6 mm needles cast on 33(33:37:37)sts and work in K1, P1 rib for 8 cm [3 in.] ending WS.
Change to 7 mm needles and work in st st inc 1 st at each end of 5th and every foll 8th row

ERICA

ERICA HOOD

until there are 47(47:51:51)sts.
Cont without shaping until work measures 44 cm [17½ in.] ending WS.

Shape top

Cast off 3 sts at beg of next 2 rows.
For sizes 86(91) cm [32(34) in.] only. Work 4 rows dec 1 st at each end of 1st row only.
For all sizes
Dec 1st at each end of next and every alt row until 7 sts rem.
Leave these sts on a spare needle.

TO MAKE UP

Join side and sleeve seams. Set in sleeves leaving left seam open to complete the neck band.

NECK BAND

With RS facing and using 6 mm needles, pick up 7 sts across left sleeve, pick and K 28 sts evenly along left side of neck, K the 1 st left on safety pin (mark this st) pick up and knit 27 sts evenly along side of neck, work 7 sts of right sleeve and then the 13 sts at back of neck. [83 sts] Work 5 rows in rib but K2tog each side of the marked st.
Cast off in rib.

To complete

Sew rem left sleeve seam and neckband seam.

DETACHABLE COLLAR OR HOOD

Using 6 mm needles cast on 89 sts and work in K1, P1 rib for 4 cm [1½ in.]
Next row WS. Make buttonhole by rib 3, cast off 2 sts, rib to end. On foll row, cast on 2 sts over buttonhole.
Work 6.5 cm [2½ in.] and make 2nd buttonhole above previous one.
Cont in rib until work measures 16 cm [6¼ in.] from beg.
Now make a third buttonhole as before *but on opposite edge of work.*
At 8 cm [3 in.] intervals make 3 more buttonholes at this edge.
Cont straight until work measures 49 cm [19 in.] from beg.
Make last buttonhole at the same side as at the *beg* of work.
Cont until work measures 58 cm [22½ in.] from beg.
Cast off in rib.

·5·

'Knickerbocker glory'

The very name conjures up tall glasses of ice cream with softly coloured hundreds and thousands sprinkled on top. This is the intended effect to a certain extent.

Making knepps or knops is a perfect way to use some of those lovely colours left over from your dyeing spree.

TO MAKE THE KNEPPS

Roll a few fibres around the first finger and roll into a knot with the thumb. Leave a 2.5 cm [1 in.] tail of loose fibres (see figs 11 and 12).

Yarn 1
Place fibres on the carders as usual and proceed to comb the wool. Before removing the wool from the carders, place several knepps over the carder at random (either all one shade or multicoloured) and continue to card once or twice more; remove and rolag in the usual way. The knepps are now within the rolag, ready for spinning.

Yarn 2
This is spun as normal without any knepps added.
Yarns 1 and 2 are plied together.
(See table overleaf.)

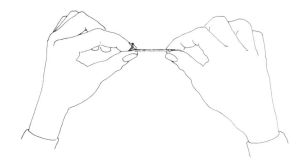

11   *Rolling fibres round finger and thumb to make knepps or knops*

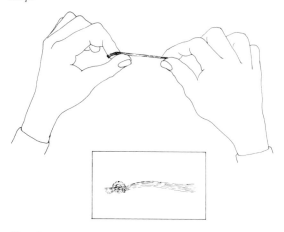

12   *Completed knepps*

AITHNE

Breed: Pick and super worsted tops
(dark grey)
Commercial worsted tops
Category: Coloured Shortwool and Down

A pure wool jacket with fashionable stand-up collar.

MATERIALS

Handspun
1. 7 threads per cm – single ply
   17 threads per in. – single ply

2. 11 threads per cm – single ply
   27 threads per in. – single ply

Nos 1 and 2 are plied together

Commercial equivalent – Aran (thin)
4.5 threads per cm
11 threads per in.

Handspun yarn
550(650) g pick and super worsted tops in dark grey (or any dark grey fleece)
25 g coloured fleece for the knepps or knops

Commercial yarn
11(13) x 50 g balls of Scheepjeswol Couture
Note the commercial yarn has the coloured wrapped around in the plying and not as given for handspun. The completed effect is very similar.

Pair each 4 mm (8) and 5 mm (6) needles
5 buttons

MEASUREMENTS

To fit bust 87-92(97-102) cm [34-36(38-40) in.]
Length 57(59) cm [22½(23¼) in.]
Sleeve seam 42 cm [16½ in.]

TENSION

15 sts and 20 rows to 10 cm [4 in.] over st st on 5 mm needles.

BACK

With 4 mm needles cast on 71(79)sts and work 9 cm [3½ in.] in K1, P1 rib.
Change to 5 mm needles and work in st st until back measures 42 cm [17 in.].

Shape armholes
Cast off 4 sts at beg of next 2 rows and 3 sts on the foll 2 rows.
Dec 1 st at each end of next 2 alt rows. [53(61)sts]
Cont straight until armhole measures 17(18) cm [6¾(7¼) in.] from beg of shaping ending RS.

Neck shaping
P19(23), cast off next 15 sts, P to end.
Cont on first set of 19(23)sts only, leaving rem sts on a stitch holder.
Dec 1 st at neck edge on the next 4(6) rows.
Cast off rem 15(17)sts.
Rejoin yarn to *inner* edge of rem 19(23)sts and complete as for first side.

'Knickerbocker Glory'

SPINNING INSTRUCTIONS													
Wheel Ratio	3:1	3½:1	4:1	4½:1	5:1	5½:1	6:1	6½:1	7:1	8:1	9:1	10:1	12:1
'Feed in' in inches per treadle													
Aran (thick)	½	½	½	¾	¾	1	1	1	1¼	1½	1½	1¾	2
4-ply	½	½	½	¾	¾	1	1	1	1¼	1½	1½	1¾	2
PLYING INSTRUCTIONS													
Per treadles per 18 inches	15	15	15	12	12	9	9	9	8	6	6	5	4½

AITHNE

RIGHT FRONT

With 4 mm needles cast on 45(49)sts and work 4 rows in K1, P1 rib.

1st buttonhole row (RS) Rib 5, cast off 2 sts, rib to end.

2nd buttonhole row Rib to last 5 sts, cast on 2 sts, rib 5.

Next row Slip 10 sts onto a safety pin and leave for the buttonhole band. Rib to end.

Cont in rib until front measures 9 cm [3½ in.] as for back.

Next row Inc 6(7)sts evenly across row. [41(46)sts]

Change to 5 mm needles and work in st st until front measures 43 cm [17 in.] ending side opposite to buttonhole band.

Shape armhole

Cast off 4 sts at beg of next row and 3 sts on the foll alt row.

Dec 1 st at same edge on next 2 alt rows.

Work 4 more rows.

Shape neck

Dec 1 st at neck edge on every row until 15(17) sts remain.

Cont straight until front measures same as back as far as shoulder.

Cast off.

LEFT FRONT

With 4 mm needles cast on 45(49)sts and work in K1, P1 rib for 7 rows.

Next row Rib 10 sts and slip these sts onto a safety pin for button band. Rib to end.

Cont in rib until work measures 9 cm [3½ in.] as for back.

Next row Inc 6(7) sts evenly across row [41(46)sts]

Change to 5 mm needles and work as for right front, reversing shapings.

SLEEVES

With 4 mm needles cast on 39(43)sts and work 8 cm [3 in.] in K1, P1 rib.

Next row Inc 4(6)sts evenly across row. [43(49)sts]

Change to 5 mm needles and work in st st inc 1 st at each end of 9th and every foll 10th row until there are 51(57)sts.

Cont straight until sleeve measures 42 cm [16½ in.] from beg.

Shape top

Cast off 4 sts at beg of next 2 rows and 2 sts on the foll 2 rows.

Dec 1 st at each end of every alt row until 15 sts remain.

Cast off 3 sts at beg of next 2 rows.

Cast off rem 9 sts.

BUTTON BAND

With 4 mm needles and RS facing, rejoin yarn to *inner* end of 10 sts on left front. Cont in K1, P1 rib until band, when *slightly* stretched, fits up neck to beg of neck shaping. Sew into place as you are knitting. Cast off in rib.

Mark off buttonhole positions for other side on this band with pins.

The 5th buttonhole is marked 4 rows down from neck edge and the rem 3 buttonholes spaced evenly in between.

BUTTONHOLE BAND

Work buttonholes as before at the positions marked by the pins on the other side.

Cast off in rib.

COLLAR

With 4 mm needles cast on 57 sts.

1st row K1, P1 rib across row.

Keeping rib as set, cast on 4 sts at beg of next 4(6) rows and 6 sts at beg of next 6 rows. [109(117)sts]

Rib 16 rows.

Cast off 6 sts at beg of next 6 rows and then 4 sts at beg of foll 4(6) rows.

Cast off rem 57 sts.

TO MAKE UP

Join shoulder and sleeve seams and set sleeves into place.

Join side seams.

Place right side of collar to right side of jacket starting and ending at top of buttonhole and button bands. Sew into place.

Fold collar in half to wrong side and sew into place.

Sew on buttons.

Whilst working on the Knickerbocker Glory chapter, a new yarn by Jaeger called *Images* appeared in the yarn shops. It is such an exciting yarn and really quite easy to attempt and so I have incorporated it here.

'KNICKERBOCKER GLORY 2'

The spinning instructions are the same as for *Aithne*.

When ready to ply the two strands together, prepare 5 different pastel shades of wool or pure mohair and pull them into long strips some 63 cm [25 in.] in length. Make a note of the colour sequence you are going to feed them in, or of course apply the colours at random. Usually, however, the most gloriously abandoned random shading was, in fact, very cleverly calculated to look that way in the first place! These strips are added to the two yarns whilst they are being plyed together.

Feed in the yarn as per plying instructions; after 4 or 5 treadles add a strip of fibres to the two yarns being plyed, but be careful to catch and trap the beginning and end of the strip safely between the plys and the rest wrapping around the two strands. This will make lovely strips of thick coloured fibres appear quite regularly throughout the garment.

NICOLA

NICOLA

Breed: Shetland
Category: Shortwool and Down
Other fibre: Mohair (goat)

Soft, delicately coloured mohair is used to make this very feminine lacy sweater with its lovely full collar.

Spinning instructions the same as *Aithne* (pp. 53-54); see plying instructions on p. 54.

MATERIALS

Handspun – mohair and wool blend
1. 7 threads per cm – single ply
   17 threads per in. – single ply

2. 11 threads per cm – single ply
   27 threads per in. – single ply
Nos 1 and 2 are plied together

Commercial equivalent – Aran (thin)
4.5 threads per cm
11 threads per in.

Handspun yarn
300(350:350:400) g
made up as to
200(250:250:300) g mohair ⎫ blended together
100 g Shetland ⎭
5 shades of coloured unspun fleece or worsted tops
Note the handspun yarn instructions were based on ideas from the commercial yarn and are not an identical repeat.

Commercial yarn
6(7:7:8) x 50 g balls of Jaeger Images

Pair each 4½ mm (7) and 5½ mm (5) and 5 mm (6) needles

TENSION

16 sts and 20 rows to 10 cm [4½ in.] over patt on 5½ mm needles.

Special abbreviation
Cross 3R – cross 3 right by K the 3rd st, P the 2nd st, then K the 1st st and let all three sts drop from left hand needle.

MEASUREMENTS

To fit bust 81(86:91:97) cm [32(34:36:38) in.]
Side seam 34 cm [13¼ in.]
Length 55.5(56.5:57:58.5) cm
[21¾(22¼:22½:23) in.]
Sleeve seam 40.5(42:43:44.5) cm
[16(16½:17:17½) in.]

BACK

** With 4½ mm needles, cast on 69(73:77:81)sts and work in crossed rib, as follows:
1st and 3rd rows * P1, K1 rep from * to last st, P1.
2nd, 4th and 6th rows * K1, P1 rep from * to last st, K1.
5th row * P1, cross 3R, rep from * to last st, P1.
Rep rows 1-6 inclusive twice more, inc 1 st at end of last row.
Change to 5½ mm needles and work in patt as follows:
1st row K1, * K2tog, yrn, rep from * to last st, K1.
2nd row P.
3rd row K2, * K2tog, yrn, rep from * to last 2 sts, K2.
4th row P.
These 4 rows form patt.
Cont in patt until back measures 35 cm [13¼ in.] ending WS.

Shape armholes
Cast off 4(5:5:5)sts at beg of next 2 rows.
Dec 1 st at each end of next and every foll alt row until 50(52:54:56)sts remain. **
Work without shaping until armhole measures 19(20:21:22) cm [7½(8:8¼:8¾) in.] ending WS.

Shape shoulders
Cast off 5 sts at beg of next 4 rows.
Cast off 4(5:5:6)sts at beg of next 2 rows. Leave 22(22:24:24)sts on a safety pin.

FRONT

Work as for back from ** to **.
Cont in patt until front measures 5 cm [2 in.] less than back to shoulder, ending WS.

Shape neck

1st row K18(19:19:20)sts, turn and complete left front and shoulder on these sts.

Leave other sts on a spare holder.

Left neck

Dec 1 st at neck edge on every row until 15(16:16:17)sts rem.

Work without shaping until front measures same as back to shoulder ending at armhole edge.

Shape shoulder

Cast off 5 sts at beg of next and foll alt row.

Cast off rem sts.

Right neck

With RS facing slip centre 14(14:16:16)sts onto a safety pin for neck. Rejoin yarn to rem 18(19:19:20)sts.

1st row K.

Dec at neck edge on next and every alt row until 15(16:16:17)sts remain.

Work until same length as back to shoulder ending at armhole edge.

Work as given for left neck.

SLEEVES

With 4½ mm needles cast on 37(39:41:41)sts and work in crossed rib for 18 rows as given for back, inc 1 st at end of last row.

Change to 5½ mm needles and work in patt, inc 1 st at each end of next and every foll 8th row until there are 44(46:48:50)sts.

Work without shaping until sleeve measures 41(42:43:44) cm [16(16½:17:17½) in.] ending WS.

Shape top

Cast off 4(5:5:5)sts at beg of next 2 rows.

Dec 1 st at each end of next and every foll alt row until 26(28:28:29)sts remain and then every row until 10(12:12:14)sts remain. Cast off.

NECK BAND AND COLLAR

Join right shoulder seam.

With 4½ mm needles, pick up and knit 13 sts down left side of neck, K14(14:16:16)sts from centre front, K13 sts up right side of neck, K across 22(22:24:24)sts from back. [62(62:66:66)sts]

Beg with K row, st st 5 cm [2 in.] ending with a P row.

Next row With P side facing inc 65(65:61:61)sts evenly across row. [127 sts]

Now work 1 complete crossed rib patt as given for back on 4½ mm needles, 1 complete patt on 5 mm needles and 3 complete patt on 5½ mm needles. Work 2 more rows in patt.

Cast off in rib.

TO MAKE UP

Join left shoulder seam.

Set in sleeves.

Join side and sleeve seams.

Join neckband and collar seams.

·6·

Dyeing-space, random and rainbow

What a wonderful world of colour this creates! All the dyeing has been done with cold water dyes and multi-purpose dyes. These little pots of colour are so useful and, rather than have large pots of one shade powder in red, green, yellow or black as is usual, one trip to the local hardware store and there is always a constant supply of new and updated shades in *small* quantities. Fashions and designs are updated so quickly that it is essential to keep in touch with colours!

In this chapter I have only used Dylon cold water dyes. The cold water dyes are colourfast and will not fade and are, therefore, the most suitable range to use. However, the Dylon multi-purpose range, to me, is far more exciting in colour but I must warn that these dyes are not colourfast inasmuch as there will be some fading after frequent washing.

Having received this warning from the manufacturers, however, I did an experiment with rainbow dyeing (see page 64) using Wensleydale fleece and both these dyes. I split the fleece into half and dyed one half with cold water dye and the other half with multi-purpose dye. When the fleece was dry I split each half into half again and then hung one section from each side in full sunlight during the summer months for several weeks. On comparing the fleece with the other two quarters, there was *no* difference in colour at all, and certainly no fading. It may be that this was explained by the use of multiple colours.

SPACE AND RANDOM DYEING

During my earlier attempts at space dyeing I found a reasonably easy way of getting a space-coloured yarn was to slip in a separate fibre, prepared in the form of a continuous roving, down the side of the preserving pan whilst doing my main batch dyeing (see fig. 13).

Although the coloured silk stripes in *Sylvia* and the silk knops in *Vera* were successfully done this way, I found the problem was to co-ordinate the dyeing sequence of colours of my main dyeing programme to allow the colours to run pleasantly through my 'foreign' yarn.

This procedure was soon abandoned but, nevertheless, it does work well.

A much more successful way involving far less hard work is as follows:

Equipment and materials
One large stainless steel preserving pan (the sort used for jam making is ideal).
Piece of plywood, half a metre [one-and-a-half feet] square, on which to prepare your fibres before sliding into the dyepot.
Glass rods or wooden spoons.
Small teaspoon. (Try and keep to the same teaspoon as a means of accurate recording.)
Notebook, pen, sticky tape and scissors for 'on the spot' recording and later adding fibres to the recording for visual reference.

Vinegar (white or brown – it will make no difference but the brown is usually cheaper).
Washing up liquid.
Dylon cold water dyes.
Wetting agent or more washing up liquid.
Large plastic bucket.

Method

For every 500 g [1.1 lb] of wool you will need:
0.85 litres [1½ pints] vinegar
1.7 litres [3 pints] water
10 squirts washing up liquid
40 minutes simmering
Each pot of dye will colour approximately 225 g [8 oz] wool; we are looking for colour in our dye programme so use at least 8 different shades per batch.
Therefore for every 500 g [1.1 lb] of wool to be dyed, use only ¼ pot of each shade.

Pre-soak your wool for approximately half-an-hour in the large bucket, with plenty of water for even wetness; use a wetting agent or a good squirt of the washing up liquid as it will help the water to soak into the wool fibres. Wool does not instantly become wet. It needs time to 'take up' the water in which it has been seeped, and a wetting agent or washing up liquid will help it absorb the water more easily.

Into the preserving pan pour the vinegar and water. Hold the squeezy bottle of washing up liquid and give ten good squirts into the pan and stir the mixture thoroughly. Remove the fibres from the bucket of water and remove as much excess water as possible.

For the random dyeing the yarn *must* be folded zigzag into the bottom of the pan, rather like a radiator, backwards and forwards carefully and neatly, sitting all the fibres in (see figs 14 and 15).

Gently press the fibres to the bottom of the pan allowing the mixture to gently soak through but not drown. The wool will sit on top anyway and not be covered by the liquid so do not worry. With a small teaspoon, pick up

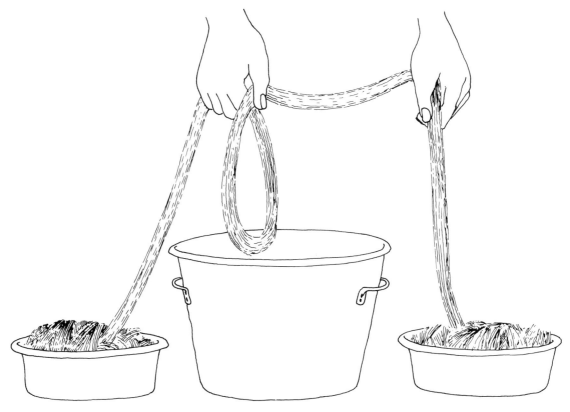

13 *'Foreign' fibres being slipped in pan for space dyeing*

¼ teaspoon of dye and with the first finger of the hand not holding the teaspoon, tap the powder evenly across the pan. This method allows for even distribution of the powder rather than trying to just shake the powder dye off the spoon. Tap the dyes in lines across the whole of the pan in stripes, fitting in all the shades evenly spaced over the pan. The powder will sit on top of the wool and look dry in most places, although sometimes water will seep onto the dyes in patches. This is normal. Gently heat the water to *simmering* point and simmer for 40 minutes. *Do not boil* and certainly do not prod or move the fibres in any way whilst it is simmering or you will break the dye sequence and probably end up with a sludge colour. However tempting, leave it alone; just keep a careful eye on not allowing the mixture to boil.

After it has simmered for 40 minutes, remove from the heat and rinse *well* and wash in the normal way in hot soapy water to remove excess dye. Dry in the normal manner.

Accurate recording is vital

Even with this method of dyeing, accurate recording *will* produce identical rovings for as many times as wanted for even the biggest of projects. The yarn for *Brenda* with the mitten, hat and scarf was done in four separate batches each time arriving at identically shaded rovings which, when laid side by side, would merge as one (see plate 10).

Note if using only 4 different shades instead of 6-8, or even 2 shades, then continue to work in stripes *repeating* the colour sequence either twice for 4 shades, or four times for 2 shades, across the pan.

14   *Zig zag fibres for random dyeing*

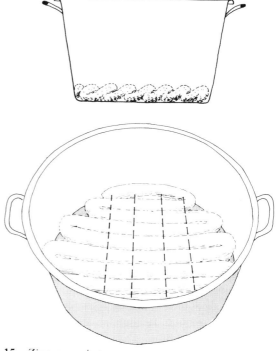

15   *Zig zag yarn in pan*

SPACE DYEING

The materials, equipment and method are very much the same as for random dyeing with the exception that the fibres are this time coiled into the bottom of the preserving pan and the dyes are tapped onto the fibres in wedges rather like cheese! The colours will slightly mingle and overlap, giving glorious middle shades to the already eight definite ones (see figs 16 and 17).

RAINBOW DYEING

This time it is a little different. Rainbow dyeing is best done with a long, silky staple fleece, like Wensleydale, or if not silky then certainly long stapled. Short staples will not work well at all.

Break off a batch of say 500 g [1.1 lb.] from the main fleece for easy handling. (This is a good way of disposing of any part of the fleece that is heavily stained or badly coloured.) Prepare the preserving pan in the normal way. There is no need to even prewash or presoak the fleece.

To handle a long-stapled fleece before washing one must be very brave indeed! There is no need but I personally would soak the fleece in cold water before dyeing, if only to use the water for my houseplants!

The method is simply to lay the fleece *tips down* into the preserving pan and scatter the dye all over the top of the fleece in the pan in batches of colour in some places and slightly mingling in others. During the simmering process the dyes will simply be dragged down to the tips in various stages of wonderful colour; this is just right for Navajo spinning and plying. (See chapter 9.) One point of warning: this is an irregular dyeing method and therefore repeat processes of similar colours will be very difficult indeed.

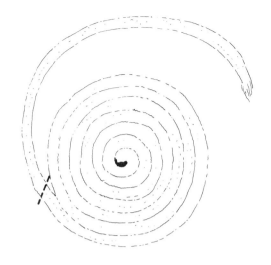

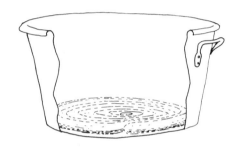

16   *Coiling the fibres for space dyeing*

17   *Coiled fibres and wedging the sections for tapping of dye powder*

1 *Grace – a finely knitted evening dress in Shetland wool with matching hip sash and head band.*

2　Katherine – elegant two-piece day suit knitted in commercial cotton or handspun cotton with Chinese Tussah silk noils.

3   *Belle – a two-tone fisherman's rib cardigan in Cheviot.*

4   Eileen – a stunning jumper with stand-up collar made from dyed worsted tops with slub contrast.

5   Felicity – a cable and lace sweater in pastel shades, threaded through with satin ribbons and with a choice of plain or picot neck finish.

6   *Foxglove – the highly textured stitch pattern gives this simple slash-neck sweater in worsted tops the designer look.*

7 *Papillon – a bouclé yarn knitted in a lovely butterfly stitch. Made from cotton, mohair and wool.*

8   Annabel – a slash-necked sweater knitted in a dropped ladder stitch and completed with elasticated cuffs and waist.

9 Ethel – a lovely soft quick-to-knit bolero made from Shetland worsted tops, samoyed dog hair and mohair.

10 Examples of colourful rainbow dyeing.

SYLVIA

Breed: Shetland
Category: Shortwool and Down
Other fibres: Tussah silk

For many years I have collected pure silk embroidery skeins mainly because of their wonderful colours! I was sure it was inevitable that one day I would knit them, and this is what I have now done! Using vibrant silk threads between pale grey wool and marrying up the shade of silk with matching satin ribbons, I designed this very attractive batwing sweater with a soft fluted neckline.

As far as the handspun version is concerned I thought it would be interesting to use space dyed silk in this design, and where a definite shade appeared in the silk stripes to match up that stripe with a similar shade of single faced satin ribbon. Therefore you alone will know what shade ribbons to look for when your garment is complete.

Do use single faced satin or a good quality ribbon; nylon is unsuitable for it will crease. Quality ribbons will remain unmoved through all the washings you care to give the garment and never crease.

(See page 26 for spinning and plying instructions.)

MATERIALS

Handspun – Shetland
10 threads per cm – single ply
25 threads per in. – single ply

Handspun – Tussah silk
10 threads per cm – single ply
25 threads per in. – single ply

Commercial equivalent – double knitting (thin)
5.5 threads per cm
14 threads per in.

Handspun yarn
300 g Shetland pale grey
100 g Tussah silk – space dyed (see page 62)

Commercial yarn
7 x 50 g balls Scheepjeswol Voluma (grey)

2 skeins of embroidery silks in each of the six shades: pale green, mustard, pink, dark green, yellow, peach

10.5 metres [34½ feet] of single faced satin ribbon
Pair each 3 mm (11) and 4 mm (8) needles
3 mm (11) circular needle 80 cm long

MEASUREMENTS

To fit bust 86-97 cm [34-38 in.]
Length 60 cm [23½ in.]
Sleeve 43 cm [17 in.]

TENSION

23 sts and 32 rows to 10 cm [4 in.] measured over striped patt using 4 mm needles.

Special abbreviations
M – main colour; C – contrast
Note this garment is worked in one piece.

Special instructions
Use knitting-in elastic with M on sleeve cuffs and lower ribs.
There are three complete changes of colour throughout this garment — 18 stripes plus the first stripe of pale green – 19 stripes in all used in following sequence: 1 – pale green, 2 – mustard, 3 – pink, 4 – dark green, 5 – yellow, and 6 – peach.

COMMENCING RIGHT SLEEVE

Using 3 mm and M and knitting-in elastic, cast on 51 sts. Work in K1, P1 rib for 6 cm [2½ in.] inc 4 sts evenly on last row. [55 sts] Break off elastic.
Change to 4 mm needles and proceed to work one complete patt as follows *at the same time* increasing 1 st at each end of 5th and every foll 5th row until there are 63 sts.

PATTERN (RS facing)

1st-7th rows St st.
8th row K.
9th row K2, * yfwd, K2tog, rep from * to end.
10th row K.
11th-18th row St st.

19th and 20th rows In C. (First stripe shade – pale green)

Knit for the stripe rows.

These 20 rows form patt.

Keeping patt correct throughout, work the stripes as set out in special instructions, *at the same time* working extra sts into patt by increasing 1 st at each end of the 3rd and every foll 4th row to 75 sts then once at each end of every alt row to 125 sts ending on WS.

Next row Cast on 2 sts at beg of next 16 rows, then 4 sts at beg of next 6 rows.   [181 sts]

Cont without shaping until 12th row of 9th stripe has been worked.

Next row Patt 88 sts. Slip these 88 sts onto a spare needle, cast off 5 sts, patt to end.

Proceed as follows on rem 88 sts:

Work 7 rows casting off 1 st at beg of 2nd and foll 4th row.   [86 sts]

Cont without shaping until 13th row of 11th stripe has been worked. Work 5 rows inc 1 st at end of next and the foll 4th row.   [88 sts]

Cont without shaping until 3rd row of the 12th stripe has been worked.

Next row Patt to end, cast on 5 sts.   [93 sts]

Break off yarn and leave these sts on a spare needle.

With WS facing, rejoin yarn to rem 88 sts left on spare needle and proceed as follows:

cast off 4 sts at beg of next row, 3 sts at beg of foll 2 alt rows, 2 sts at beg of foll alt row and 1 st at beg of foll 3 alt rows.   [73 sts]

Cont without shaping until 9th row of 11th stripe has been worked.

Cast on 1 st at beg of next and foll 2 alt rows, 2 sts at beg of foll alt row, 3 sts at beg of foll 2 alt rows and 4 sts at beg of foll alt row.   [88 sts]

Next row Patt to end, patt across 93 sts left on spare needle.   [181 sts]

Cont without shaping until 10th row of 14th stripe has been worked. Cast off 4 sts at beg of next 6 rows, and 2 sts at beg of next 16 rows.

Dec 1 st at each end of next and every foll alt row until 75 sts remain, then every foll 4th row until 55 sts remain.

Work 3 rows without shaping.

(The 19th stripe is now complete.)

Work 18 more rows in patt.

Change to 3 mm and M. With knitting-in elastic work in K1, P1 rib for 6 cm [2½ in.] dec 4 sts evenly across first row.

Cast off in rib.

LOWER BORDERS (both alike)

With RS facing and 3 mm needles and M pick up and knit 95 sts evenly along lower edge. Join in knitting-in elastic and work in K1, P1 rib for 13 cm [5 in.]. Cast off loosely in rib.

NECK BAND

With RS facing and 3 mm circular needle and M, pick up and knit 118 sts evenly all round neck edge and work in patt as follows:

1st round Eyelet row K2, * yfwd, K2tog, rep from * to end.

2nd round P.

3rd round * P5, K1, rep from * to end.

4th round * P5, yrn, K1, yon, rep from * to end.

5th round * P5, K3, rep from * to end.

6th round * P5, yrn, K3, yon, rep from * to end.

7th round * P5, K5, rep from * to end.

8th round * P5, yrn, K5, yon, rep from * to end.

9th round * P5, K7, rep from * to end.

10th round * P5, yrn, K7, yon, rep from * to end.

11th round * P5, K9, rep from * to end.

Cast off.

TO MAKE UP

Sew up side and sleeve seams.

Make a cord and thread through eyelet holes at neck.

SYLVIA

S and Z

So far all the yarns in this book have been spun in one direction (forwards) and plyed in one direction (backwards).

Many of the fancy yarns would disintegrate if spinning of the fibres was all done this way. Therefore there are some yarns that need to be spun in the opposite way to each other so that one will tighten its hold on the other and not disintegrate or slowly unravel while in the final stages of being plyed. This spinning is called S and Z.

An easy way of remembering S and Z spin is to write an imaginary S or Z over the top of your wheel, as if your hand was turning the wheel. In tracing the Z you will see that the hand goes from left to right and to start your wheel this way will make it go forward (clockwise); similarly, to write the imaginary S the hand movement would go from right to left thus making the wheel go backwards (anticlockwise) (see figs 18 and 19).

So now you have control over the thickness of your yarn and can understand how to colour it. Now the final step is whether to spin the yarn Z forwards or S backwards as you move on to the world of slub, knop, bouclé, curled loop, spiral and colour.

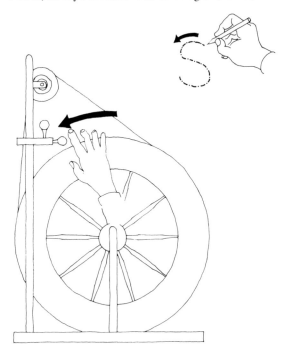

18 *S twist – clockwise*

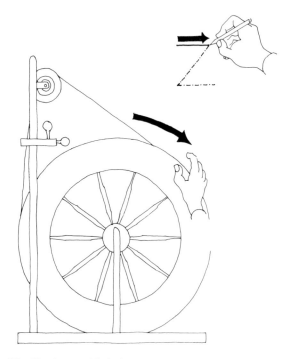

19 *Z twist – anticlockwise*

·8·

Slub and wrapped slub

SLUB

The ability to achieve a slub yarn usually comes naturally to a beginner, who is concentrating all her worth on trying to get a smooth yarn and is constantly being reminded by her tutor on the splendour of her textured yarn! When a smooth yarn has been achieved, she is then required to return to her earlier efforts in a more controlled way and produce that textured yarn again – only to find those natural abilities have now disappeared!

However, all is not lost for slub is quite easy to achieve. The main yarn of the next garment is Icelandic, as is the multi-coloured slub contrast, and therefore good preparation is vital. So turn to page 75 and follow the instructions and illustrations as for the preparation and spinning of the main yarn and preparation, only of the multi-coloured slub yarn instead.

TO SPIN SLUB

Feed in the yarn at the treadles per 18 inches as instructed for approximately 4-6 treadles and then make a slub. This is achieved by pinching the fibres with one hand and holding onto this chunk (see fig. 20), whilst moving down the roving in the usual way. As one's hold is released (see fig. 21), the twist in the normal thread jumps behind the slub to the normal spin again (see fig. 22) and the slub is made (see fig. 23).

Treadle *slowly* and work slowly and methodically throughout this procedure: 4-6 treadles, slub, 4-6 treadles, slub and so on.

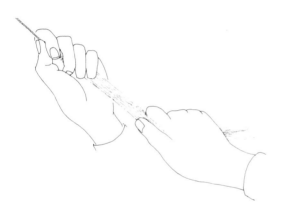

20   *Clamping fibres with left hand to make slub*

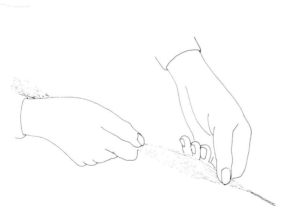

21   *Hand releases clamped clump*

PLY INSTRUCTIONS

Hold the slub yarn in the left hand, lazy kate right down by left foot underneath the orifice, and the wrap yarn in the right hand. Ply S. *Hold both hands near to the orifice* plying in together regularly (see fig. 24), but for every slub bring hand holding the wrap yarn in the right hand out immediately parallel (see fig. 25) so that yarn wraps all the way round the slub and holds it safely. *Treadle slowly* (see fig. 26).

Note a wheel with a large orifice and large cup hooks will be a great help in producing the coming yarns. If you own an Ashford Wheel then you will find a Jumbo Flyer very helpful. If the orifice of your wheel is quite large, then replace the small cup hooks that feed the yarn evenly onto the bobbins with large ones to help the slub yarn move freely past them onto the bobbin.

22   *Move down fibres in normal manner*

23   *Spin jumps past slub and slub is made*

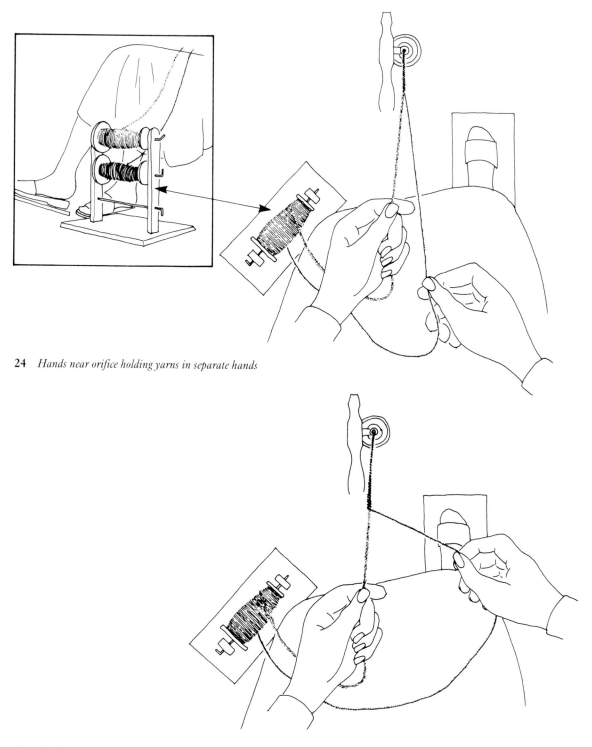

24 *Hands near orifice holding yarns in separate hands*

25 *Hands approaching slub, move up parallel to encase it*

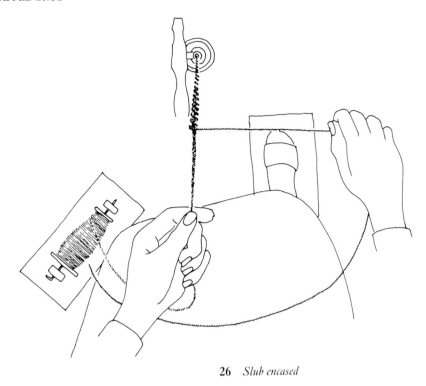

26 *Slub encased*

EILEEN

Other fibres: Dyed worsted tops

This is a stunning way of using your first attempts at random dyeing. The main yarn in Icelandic means that only 400 g is used for the slub contrast and yet colours flow from sleeve to sleeve. An attractive double collar completes the design.

MATERIALS

Handspun – main yarn spun Z
3.5 threads per cm – single ply
9 threads per in. – single ply

Commercial equivalent – Icelandic or Lopi yarn
This is a single ply yarn
3.5 threads per cm
9 threads per in.

Handspun – contrast spun S (Aran thickness)
8 threads per cm – single ply
20 threads per in. – single ply
This will be the same shade as the main yarn for colour co-ordination
Pinched slub yarn spun Z
3.5 threads per cm
9 threads per in.

Commercial yarn – chunky slub yarn
2.0 threads per cm
5 threads per in.

Handspun yarn
700(750) g main yarn
Contrast is made up of:
400(400) g of coloured dyed slub
200(200) g Aran (thin)
1 pot each of Dylon cold water dye shades:
A3 Lilac, A6 Moon Blue, A15 Tartan Green, A20 Radiant Pink, A22 Sahara Sun and A23 Bahama Blue (see dyeing wheel illustration fig. 27)

Commercial yarn

4(5) x 100 g hanks Scheepjeswol Flammé Colori
6(7) x 100 g balls Samband Lopi

Pair each 5 mm (6) and 6 mm (4) knitting needles

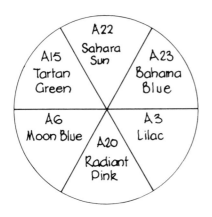

27 *Dye chart for EILEEN*

MEASUREMENTS

To fit bust 97(102) cm [38(40) in.]
Length 50(52) cm [19½(20½) in.]
Sleeve 46 cm [18 in.]

TENSION

16 sts and 26 rows to 10 cm [4 in.] measured over patt on 6 mm needles.

Special abbreviations

Tw2R – twist 2 right by knitting second stitch passing in *front* of work, then knit first stitch.
Tw2L – twist 2 left by knitting second stitch passing *behind* first stitch, then knit first stitch.
M – main; C – contrast

BACK

Using 5 mm needles and M, cast on 65(71)sts and work in K1, P1 rib for 8 cm [3 in.] ending with RS.
Next row Rib to end, inc 9(11)sts evenly across row. [74(82)sts]

Lopi

MAIN yarn – Icelandic spun Z

SPINNING INSTRUCTIONS

Wheel Ratio	3:1	3½:1	4:1	4½:1	5:1	5½:1	6:1	6½:1	7:1	8:1	9:1	10:1	12:1
'Feed in' in inches per treadle	1½	1¾	2	2¼	2½	2½	3	3	3½	4	4½		

PLYING INSTRUCTIONS	There are no plying instructions – this is a single ply yarn

ARAN contrast yarn – wrap yarn spun S

SPINNING INSTRUCTIONS

Wheel Ratio	3:1	3½:1	4:1	4½:1	5:1	5½:1	6:1	6½:1	7:1	8:1	9:1	10:1	12:1
'Feed in' in inches per treadle	½-¾	¾	¾	¾	1	1	1¼	1¼	1½	1¾	2	2¼	2½

PLYING INSTRUCTIONS	There are no plying instructions at this stage

LOPI contrast yarn – pinched slub yarn spun Z – thick coloured

SPINNING INSTRUCTIONS

Wheel Ratio	3:1	3½:1	4:1	4½:1	5:1	5½:1	6:1	6½:1	7:1	8:1	9:1	10:1	12:1
'Feed in' in inches per treadle	1½	1¾	2	2¼	2½	2½	3	3	3½	4	4½		

PLYING INSTRUCTIONS	There are no plying instructions at this stage

Note: this yarn is suitable for *Brenda* and accessories, and *Brenda* yarn for *Eileen*.

EILEEN

Change to 6 mm needles and C.
Knit 2 rows.
Work in patt as follows:
1st, 3rd and 5th rows In M, K1, * P3, ybk, Sl2P, P3, rep from * to last st, K1.
2nd, 4th and 6th rows In M, K1, * K3, yfd, Sl2P, K3, rep from * to last st, K1.
7th row Change to C, K1 * P2, Tw2R, Tw2L, P2, rep from * to last st, K1.
8th row In C, K.
9th, 11th and 13th rows In M, P1 * ybk, Sl1P, yfd, P6, ybk, Sl1P, rep from * to last st, K1.
10th, 12th and 14th rows In M, K1, * yfd, Sl1P, ybk, K6, yfd, Sl1P, rep from * to last st, K1.
15th row Change to C, K1, * Tw2L, P4, Tw2R, rep from * to last st, K1.
16th row In C, K.
These 16 rows form patt.
Work in patt until work measures 12 cm [4½ in.]. Place a coloured marker at each end of last row to indicate armholes.
Cont straight in patt until work measures 49(51) cm [19(20) in.] ending with WS.

Shape neck

Next row Patt 25(28)sts, cast off 24(26)sts, patt to end.
Now work each side of neck edge by using separate balls of yarn for each side and a separate 6 mm needle.
Note alternatively, you can first work one side and then the other to match, reversing shaping.
Next row Patt to end.
Next row Cast off 9 sts at neck edge, patt to end.
Next row Cast off rem 16(19)sts for shoulder.

FRONT

Work as for back until work measures 45(47) cm [18(18½) in.] ending with WS.

Shape neck

Either both sides together or alternatively reversing shaping as follows:

Next row Patt 31(34)sts, cast off 12(14)sts, patt to end.
Cast off at neck edge on alternate rows 4 sts once, 3 sts 3 times, and 2 sts once. Cont until work measures 50(52) cm [19¾(20½) in.].
Cast off rem 16(19)sts for shoulders.

SLEEVES

With 5 mm needles and M, cast on 35(38)sts and work in K1, P1 rib for 6 cm [2½ in.] ending with RS.
Next row Rib to end inc 15(18)sts evenly across row. [50(56)sts]
Change to 6 mm needles and C. K 2 rows.
Now work first row of patt as given for back.
Cont working in patt as set *at the same time* inc 1 st at each end of every 4th row until there are 100(106)sts, working extra sts into patt.
Cont until work measures 46 cm [18 in.]. Cast off.

NECK BAND

Sew left shoulder seam. Using 5 mm needles and M, pick up and knit 60(65)sts evenly around neck edge. Work 5 cm [2 in.] in K1, P1 rib. Change to 6 mm needles. Work 1 row in rib. Cast off loosely in rib.

COLLAR

With 5 mm needles and M, cast on 77(80)sts. Work in K1, P1 rib for 10 cm [4 in.]. Change to 6 mm needle and cast off loosely in rib.

TO MAKE UP

Join right shoulder and neck seams.
Fold sleeves in half and set between the coloured markers. Sew into place.
Join side and sleeve seams.
Sew cast on edge of collar to inside of neck band.

WRAPPED SLUB

The speed at which this yarn is put together means the bulk of the work will be in the preparation of the multi-coloured wrap yarn, so it is worth while spending some time pulling the roving out to the thickness required and letting it drop into the bucket, for smooth flow of yarn onto the wheel. It will be vulnerable to separation at this time. If it does break, simply lay the fibres on top of each other, pull out slightly to the right thickness and proceed as before.

Once the roving has been random dyed the colours will be very bright. As you break down the roving into batts and pull them out ready for spinning, the fibres take on a much softer hue. It is at this stage of softness that you will be able to pick the shade of the final wrap to complement and complete the yarn.

TO SPIN SLUB

Pull out multi-coloured roving to 1 cm (½ in.) thickness, constantly checking thickness as you pile these fibres into the bucket by laying the roving onto a wooden ruler and measuring it. Tie a cotton core onto the bobbin and attach the roving to this core. With the cotton core in the left hand and the roving in the right hand, proceed to spin slowly S, wrapping the roving around the core, covering it completely (see fig. 28).

The core should be down as near to the orifice as possible by your left leg, and the bucket by your right-hand side.

TO PLY

Hold the wrapped slub in the left hand and the final wrap in the right hand and working Z let the slub wrap the wrap rather than the other way round, working fairly quickly near the orifice to avoid overplying (see fig. 29). Watch for the yarn catching on the cup hooks. If they should, ease it off and proceed. As the bobbin fills, which it does rapidly, ease on the brakeband for a slightly faster pull-in.

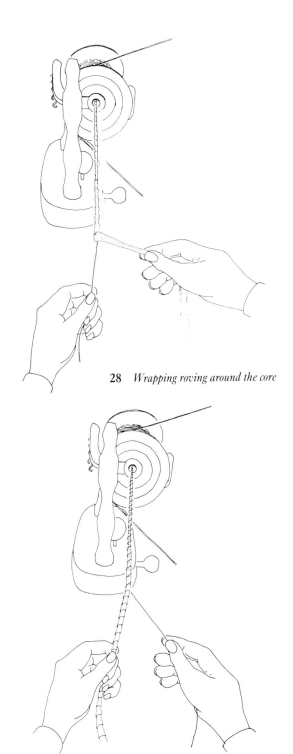

28 *Wrapping roving around the core*

29 *Hold slub in left hand and wrap in right letting the slub wrap the wrap*

BRENDA

Category: Dyed worsted tops

Gloriously coloured casual jacket with shawl collar and patch pockets with pretty matching hat, scarf and mittens. All set for those winter months ahead.

MATERIALS

Handspun
Wrap – roving not spun
Roving to be pulled up to 1 cm [½ in.] thickness.
Ply yarn – spun S (Aran)
8 threads per cm – single ply
20 threads per in. – single ply

Commercial equivalent – chunky slub yarn
2.0 threads per cm
5 threads per in.

Handspun yarn
COAT
(A) 800 g dyed commercial worsted tops
(B) 250 g dyed commercial worsted tops dyed with Dylon cold water dye shade A20 Radiant Pink
1 pot each of Dylon cold water dye shades:
A2, A11, A13, A15, A19, A20, A27, A30 (see dyeing wheel illustration fig. 30)
(C) 200 g fine cotton for core
HAT
80 g of (A)
20 g of (B)
20 g of (C)

MITTENS
80 g of (A)
20 g of (B)
20 g of (C)
SCARF
350 g of (A)
50 g of (B)
50 g of (C)

Commercial yarn
COAT
11 x 100 g hanks Scheepjeswol Flammé Colori
HAT
1 x 100 g hank Scheepjeswol Flammé Colori
MITTENS
1 x 100 g hank Scheepjeswol Flammé Colori
SCARF
4 x 100 g hanks Scheepjeswol Flammé Colori

Pair each 8 mm (6) and 6 mm (4) needles
7 buttons

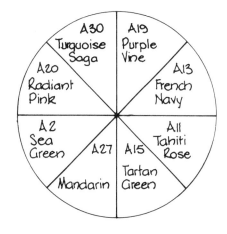

30   *Dye chart for BRENDA*

Wrapped slub

SPINNING INSTRUCTIONS

Wheel Ratio	3:1	3½:1	4:1	4½:1	5:1	5½:1	6:1	6½:1	7:1	8:1	9:1	10:1	12:1
'Feed in' in inches per treadle													
Yarn A: Ply spun S	1¼	1½	1½	1¾	2	2	2½	2½	3	3	3½	4	

Yarn B: Wrap	This is a roving and is not spun – the roving must be pulled out to 1 cm [½ in.] thickness. See method and plying instructions.
Yarn C: Core	A fine commercial cotton.

PLYING INSTRUCTIONS	There are no plying instructions at this stage

Note: this yarn is also suitable for *Eileen*, and *Eileen* yarn for *Brenda*.

79

COAT

MEASUREMENTS

All round underarm 112 cm [44 in.]
Length 57.5 cm [22½ in.]
Sleeve seam 51 cm [20 in.] including 5 cm [2 in.] fold back

TENSION

10 sts and 14 rows to 10 cm [4 in.] on 8 mm needles.

Special abbreviations

M1 – make one by picking up loop lying horizontal to next stitch and purling into back of it.

BACK AND FRONT

With 8 mm needles cast on 100 sts and work 5 cm [2 in.] in garter st (every row knit).
Next row P.
Change to reversed st st (purl on right side of work).
Work straight until work measures 18 cm [7 in.].

Pocket placing

P5, place a coloured marker, P14, place a second coloured marker. Work to last 19 sts, place a third coloured marker, P14, place fourth and last coloured marker, P5.
Continue in reversed st st until work measures 25.5 cm [14 in.].
With RS facing separate for back as follows:
Slip 25 sts onto separate needle, P50, slip next 25 sts onto a separate needle.
Work on back 50 sts straight for 21.5 cm [8½ in.] from separation.

Shape shoulders

Cast off 12 sts at beg of next 2 rows.
Cast off rem 26 sts.
Rejoin separate yarns to left and right fronts and work simultaneously.
Work 8 cm [3 in.] in reversed st st.

Shape neck

Dec 1 st at neck edge for the next 16 rows. [9 sts]
Work 4 rows straight.
Cast off.

SLEEVES

Using 8 mm needles cast on 45 sts. Work 7 rows in garter st.
8th row P.
Work in reversed st st for 70 rows. (51 cm) [20 in.]
Cast off very loosely.

BORDER AND HALF COLLAR

With 8 mm needles cast on 5 sts. Work in garter st throughout for 43 cm [17 in.] stitching work into place as you go.

Shape collar

Inc 1 st at beg of next row and at the same edge on each row until there are 16 sts. Work straight on these sts for 24 cm [9½ in.].
Cast off.

BUTTONHOLE BORDER AND HALF COLLAR

With 8 mm needles cast on 5 sts.
Work in garter st for 2 rows.
Buttonhole row K2, yrn, K2tog, K1.
Work 10 rows.
Rep buttonhole row.
Cont working buttonholes as before until 7 buttonholes are complete. 43 cm [17 in.]
Shape collar as before.

POCKETS (make 2)

Using 8 mm needles cast on 16 sts and garter st 20 rows.
Cast off.

TO MAKE UP

Sew shoulder seams.
Sew collar pieces together neatly across back of neck.
Set in sleeves and sew sleeve seams.
Fold back the 7 rows of garter st on the sleeve and secure at seam.
Line pockets up to markers (they will slightly overlap). Stitch into place.
Sew on buttons.

BRENDA WITH HAT SCARF AND MITTENS

HAT

TENSION

10 sts and 17 rows to 10 cm [4 in.] on 6 mm knitting needles.

With 6 mm needles cast on 54 sts.
Garter st (every row knit) for 12 rows.
Starting with P row change to reverse st st and work 20 rows.
Dec for crown as follows:
P2, (P2tog, P8) 5 times, P2.
Work 1 row.
P2, (P2tog, P7) 5 times, P2.
Work 1 row.
P2, (P2tog, P6) 5 times, P2.
Cont to dec 5 sts every alt row for 5 more dec.
Next row P2tog across row.
Break yarn, draw up sts, and sew up seam.

MITTENS

TENSION

As for hat

With 6 mm needles cast on 20 sts and garter st 16 rows, inc 1 st at each end of the last row. [22 sts]
Beg with P row change to reversed st st and work 6 rows.

Shape gusset
P10, M1, P2, M1, P10.
Work 1 row.
P10, M1, P4, M1, P10.
Work 1 row.

Divide for thumb
P16, turn, cast on 1 st, K7, turn.
Work 8 rows on these 7 sts.

To shape thumb
P2tog, P3, P2tog.
Draw thread through rem 5 sts and sew up thumb seam.
Beg at thumb base, pick up and knit 5 sts across thumb base, P10. 25 sts.
Work 11 rows in reversed st st.

Shape top
P2tog, P1, rep to end.
Work 1 row.
Rep last 2 rows twice more.
Cast off sts repeating first row.

TO MAKE UP

Sew up seam.

SCARF

TENSION

As for coat.

With 8 mm needles cast on 22 sts. Work in garter st for 104 cm [72 in.]. Cast off.

Optional
Cut 25 cm [10 in.] strands of yarn and thread 2 strands together along short ends of scarf approx 2.5 cm [1 in.] apart.

Navajo ply-plain and coloured

PLAIN

A true Aran yarn is three-stranded which, when plyed together, will give the good round yarn that is necessary for Aran knitting. This can be achieved by spinning three separate bobbins and holding all three strands very firmly and evenly when plying, otherwise the result will look uneven.

An excellent alternative would be to Navajo ply, which is a method of making a three-ply yarn from only one bobbin! This also enables one to use up all surplus yarn with no leftovers on subsequent bobbins.

TO SPIN

Follow the spinning instructions given below.

TO PLY

To ply is as easy as making a continuous chain stitch, just as in crochet.

Tie the single yarn to the bobbin and make a loop in front of orifice (beginning of chain stitch), pull this loop out to 12-15 cm [5-6 in.] wide and proceed to ply anticlockwise S. At the same time put the finger and thumb of your right hand into the loop and draw the thread through to make a second loop. Gently slide fingers of the left hand up the yarn, which is now 3-ply to the beginning of the second loop, and feed yarn in onto the bobbin. Now repeat the process throughout. Until confidence flows, just practise pulling out the loops – say three at 6 inches in width. You now have the 18 inch span usual for plying and can feed that length onto the bobbin after the correct amount of pedals for your ratio. In time hands and feet will synchronise and the loops will get much bigger than 6 inches!

Navajo ply

SPINNING INSTRUCTIONS													
Wheel Ratio	3:1	3½:1	4:1	4½:1	5:1	5½:1	6:1	6½:1	7:1	8:1	9:1	10:1	12:1
'Feed in' in inches per treadle	½-¾	¾	¾	¾	1	1	1¼	1¼	1½	1½	1¾	2	2½
PLYING INSTRUCTIONS													
Per treadles per 18 inches	22	18	18	18	14	14	11	11	9	9	8	7	5

▨▨▨ THOMAS ▨▨▨

Breed: Masham
Category: Mountain and Hill

A very attractive Aran sweater with classic round neck and knitted in sporting check stitch which looks complicated but, in fact, is a simple slip stitch.

MATERIALS

Handspun – Masham
8 threads per cm – single ply
21 threads per in. – single ply

Commercial equivalent – (when three-plyed)
Aran (thick)
4 threads per cm
10 threads per in.

Handspun yarn
150(175:225) g dyed Masham (blue) for main yarn
100(150:200) g light grey Masham for contrast yarn
1 pot Dylon cold water dye A28 Riviera Blue

Commercial yarn
4(5:6) x 40 g balls Sunbeam Mountaineer for main shade
2(3:4) x 50 g balls Sunbeam Aran Tweed for contrast shade

Note Aran Knit, Mountaineer and Aran Tweed yarns are all interchangeable. Although the Sunbeam yarn is of Aran quality, it has been three-plyed and *not* Navajo plyed.

Pair each 4 mm (8) and 5 mm (6) needles

MEASUREMENTS

To fit chest 56(61:66) cm [22(24:26) in.]
All round underarms 58.5(63:70) cm
[23(24¾:27½) in.]
Side seams 21.5(25:28.5) cm
[8½(9¾:11¼) in.]
Length from top of shoulder 35(39:43 cm)
[13¾(15¼:17) in.]
Sleeve seam 28.5(31:34) cm
[11¼(12¼:13¼) in.]

TENSION

18 sts and 28 rows to 10 cm [4 in.] on 5 mm needles over patt.

Special abbreviations
M – main; C – contrast; wyif – with yarn in front; wyab – with yarn at back.

BACK

With 4 mm needles and M, cast on 52(56:62)sts and work in K1, P1 rib for 5 cm [2 in.].
Change to 5 mm needles and work in sporting check pattern as follows:
1st row (RS) In C, K.
2nd row With C, K0(3:0), (K1, P1) twice, K1, * P2, K1, P1, K1 rep from * to last 2(3:2)sts, P2(3:2).
3rd row In M, K1(3:1) * K5, (Sl1 wyab, K1) twice, Sl1 wyab, rep from * to last 1(3:1)sts, K1(3:1).
4th rows With M, K1(3:1) * (Sl1 wyif, K1) twice, Sl1 wyif, K5, rep from * to last 1(3:1)sts, K1(3:1).
5th row With C, K.
6th row With C, K1(3:1) * (P1, K1) twice, Pl, K5, rep from * to last 1(3:1)sts, K1(3:1).
7th, 8th, 9th, 10th, 11th and 12th rows Rep 3rd, 4th, 5th and 6th rows, then 3rd and 4th rows again.
13th and 14th rows With C, rep 1st and 2nd rows.
15th row With M, K1(3:1) * (Sl1 wyab, K1) twice, Sl1 wyab, K5, rep from * to last 1(3:1)sts, K1(3:1).
16th row With M, K1(3:1), * K5, (Sl1 wyif, K1) twice, Sl1 wyif, rep from * to last 1(3:1)sts, K1(3:1).
17th row With C, K.
18th row With C, K1(3:1), * K5 (P1, K1) twice, P1, rep from * to last 1(3:1)sts, K1(3:1).
19th, 20th, 21st, 22nd, 23rd and 24th rows Rep 15th, 16th, 17th and 18th rows, then 15th and 16th rows again.
These 24 rows form patt.
Cont straight until back measures 21.5(24.5:28.5) cm [8½(9¾:11¼) in.] ending WS.

THOMAS AND JAMES

Shape armholes

Cast off 2(3:4) at beg of next 2 rows keeping patt correct.

Dec 1 st at each end of next and the foll 5 alt rows.   [36(38:40)sts]

Work straight until armhole measures 11.5(12:12.5) cm [4½(4¾:5) in.].

Shape shoulders

Cast off 3 sts at beg of next 4 rows, then 3(4:5)sts on the foll 2 rows. Leave rem 18 sts on a stitch holder.

FRONT

Work as for back until armhole shaping has been completed.   [36(38:40)sts]

Patt 6(8:10) rows.

Divide for neck

Patt 14(15:15), turn. Leave rem sts on a stitch holder.

Working on these 14(15:15)sts shape neck as follows:

Dec 1 st at neck edge on next and 5 foll alt rows.   [8(9:9)sts]

Patt 15 rows.

(*Note* work 1 extra row when working other side.)

Shape shoulders

Cast off 3 sts at beg of next and foll alt row.

Work 1 row.

Cast off rem 2(3:3)sts.

With RS facing slip 8(8:10)sts onto a stitch holder. Rejoin yarn to rem 14(15:15)sts and complete as for other side remembering extra row.

SLEEVES

Work in M only.

With 4 mm needles cast on 30(32:34)sts and work in K1, P1 rib for 5 cm [2 in.].

Inc row Inc 12(14:14)sts evenly across row. [42(46:48)sts]

Change to 5 mm needles and work in st st throughout.

Work straight until sleeve seam measures 28.5(31:34) cm. [11¾(12¼:13¼) in.]

Shape sleeve top

Cast off 2(3:4)sts at beg of next 2 rows, then dec 1 st at each end of the next row and the foll 2(3:3) alt rows.   [32 sts]

Purl 1 row.

Cast off 2 sts at beg of next 10 rows. Cast off rem 12 sts.

NECK BAND

Join right shoulder seam.

With RS facing in M with 4 mm needles, pick up and knit 16 sts from row ends of left front. Knit across 8(8:10)sts at centre front; pick up and knit 16 sts from row ends of right front and finally 18 sts across back neck.   [58(58:60)sts]

Work 8 rows in K1, P1 rib. Cast off loosely in rib.

TO MAKE UP

Join left shoulder seam and neck band.

Set in sleeves.

Join side and sleeve seams.

JAMES

Breed: Masham
Category: Mountain and Hill

Man's sweater in sporting check. Like father, like son. Similar style Aran sweater in same sporting check stitch. But by slightly changing the colour sequence of the two yarns on only one row it radically changes the completed look. Therefore the combinations of colours in this design and *Thomas* are endless, simply by changing the colour of the yarn and not the stitch!

Spinning and plying instructions as for *Thomas* (page 83).

MATERIALS

Handspun – Masham
8 threads per cm – single ply
21 threads per in. – single ply
This yarn to be Navajo plyed or 3-ply

Commercial equivalent – Aran (thick)
4 threads per cm
10 threads per in.

Handspun yarn
750(800) g Masham dark grey
200(250) g Masham light grey

Commercial yarn
15(16) x 50 g balls Sunbeam Aran Tweed for main shade
4(5) x 50 g balls Sunbeam Aran Knit for contrast shade.
Note Aran Knit, Mountaineer and Aran Tweed are all interchangeable.
Although the Sunbeam yarn is of Aran quality, it has been three-plyed and *not* Navajo plyed

Pair each 4 mm (8) and 5 mm (6) needles
Stitch holder

MEASUREMENTS

To fit chest 102(107) cm [40(42) in.]
Length from top of shoulder 67(68) cm
[26½(26¾) in.]
Sleeve seam 46(47) cm [18(18½) in.]

TENSION

18 sts and 28 rows to 10 cm [4 in.] on 5 mm needles over patt.

Special abbreviations
M – main; C – contrast; wyif – with yarn in front: wyab – with yarn at back.

BACK

With 4 mm needles and M, cast on 92(98)sts and work in K1, P1 rib for 8 cm [3 in.].
For second size only
Inc 4 sts evenly across row.   [102 sts]
For both sizes
Change to 5 mm needles and work in patt as follows:
1st row Still in M, K.
2nd row With C, (K1,P1) twice, K1, * P2, K1, P1, K1, rep from * to last 2 sts, P2.
3rd row With C, K1, * K5, (Sl1 wyab, K1) twice, Sl1 wyab, rep from * to last st, K1.
4th row With C, K1, * (Sl1 wyif, K1) twice, Sl1 wyif, K5, rep from * to last st, K1.
5th row With M, K.
6th row With M, K1, * (P1, K1) twice, Pl, K5, rep from * to last st, K1.
7th, 8th, 9th, 10th, 11th and 12th rows Rep 3rd, 4th, 5th and 6th rows, and then 3rd and 4th rows again.
13th and 14th rows With M, rep 1st and 2nd rows.
15th row With C, K1, * (Sl1 wyab, K1) twice, Sl1 wyab, K5, rep from * to last st, K1.
16th row With C, K1, * K5, (Sl1 wyif, K1) twice, Sl1 wyif, rep from * to last st, K1.
17th row With M, K.
18th row With M, K1, * K5, (P1,K1) twice, P1, rep from * to last st, K1.
19th, 20th, 21st, 22nd, 23rd and 24th rows Rep 15th, 16th, 17th and 18th rows, then 15th and 16th rows again.
These 24 rows form patt.
Work straight until back measures 43 cm [17 in.] from beg ending WS.

Shape armholes
Cast off 5(6)sts at beg next 2 rows. Dec 1 st at each end of next 3 rows and then each end of foll 5 alt rows.   [66(74)sts]

Work straight until work measures 24(25) cm [9½(9¾) in.] from beg of armhole shaping.

Shape shoulders

Cast off 4 sts at beg of next 6 rows.
Then cast off 4(7)sts at beg next 2 rows.
Leave rem 34(36)sts on a stitch holder.

FRONT

Work as for back until 18 rows less than back to shoulder shaping.

Shape front neck

Patt 22(23), turn, leave rem sts on spare needle.
* Dec 1 st at neck edge on next and foll 6(7) alt rows.   [15 sts]
Work straight until front is same length as back to shoulder ending armhole edge.

Shape shoulder

Cast off 4 sts at beg of next and foll 2 alt rows.
Work 1 row.
Cast off rem 3 sts.
With RS facing slip 22(28)sts onto a stitch holder. Rejoin yarn and work to match first side from * to end.

SLEEVES

Knitted in M and st st throughout.
With 4 mm needles and M, cast on 44(48)sts and work in K1, P1 rib for 8 cm [3 in.].
Change to 5 mm needles and continue in M and st st throughout inc 1 st at each end of the next and every foll 6th row until 76(78)sts.
Work straight until sleeve measures 46(47) cm. [18(18½) in.] from beg.

Shape top

Cast off 5 sts at beg of next 2 rows.
Dec 1 st at each end of next 3 rows.
Dec 1 st each end of every foll alt row to 28 sts.
Work 1 row.
Cast off 3 sts at beg of next 6 rows. Cast off rem 10 sts.

NECK BAND

Join left shoulder seam.
With RS facing and using 4 mm needles and M knit up 34(36) sts from stitch holder at back neck, pick up and K 20 sts from left front neck, K 22(28) sts from stitch holder at centre front neck, pick up and K 20 sts from right front neck.   [96(104)sts]
Work in K1, P1 rib for 5 cm [2 in.]. Cast off loosely in rib.

TO MAKE UP

Join right shoulder seam and neck band. Fold neck band in half to wrong side and stitch down.
Set in sleeves.
Join side and sleeve seams.

▩▩▩ COLOUR ▩▩▩

Apart from the pleasure of only having always to spin just one bobbin for our 3-ply yarn, Navajo plying is also an excellent way of keeping random spun or rainbow dyed colours separated precisely and not to have several shades overlapping, which would inevitably happen when plying two yarns together. Another way, of course, would be to ply one multi-coloured strand with a plain coloured strand but this would naturally result in the vibrant colours being diminished.

Follow the spinning and plying instructions, as before, and by now you should have obtained control over the pull out of your yarn into the chain loops and be able to make them bigger or smaller. This is precisely what to do: make the chains as large as you wish but immediately there is a changeover of colour, pull the loop through only enough to *stop there* at the colour change. No matter how hard you look at the large or small loops of the completed yarn the break to make fresh loops does not show, and the colours stay separated.

FELICITY

Breed: Pick and Super
             Miscellaneous commercial
             worsted tops.
Category: Shortwool and Down

An absolutely stunning all-in-one cable and lace sweater in lovely subtle shades of pale green, primrose, dawn pink and lilac, threaded throughout with satin ribbons. Pure pleasure to wear at any time. With alternative instructions for a plain or picot edged neck band. (Spinning and plying instructions as for *Thomas*, page 83.)

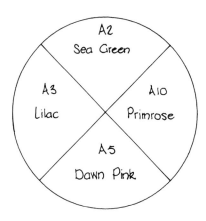

31   *Dye chart for FELICITY*

MATERIALS

Handspun – worsted tops
8 threads per cm – single ply
21 threads per in. – single ply

Commercial equivalent – double knitting (thick)
4 threads per cm
10 threads per in.

Handspun yarn
500 g space dyed worsted tops
1 pot each Dylon cold water dyes shades:
A2 Sea Green, A10 Primrose, A5 Dawn Pink and A3 Lilac (see dyeing wheel illustration fig. 31)

Commercial yarn
10 x 40 g balls Georges Picaud No. 1 Country
Note I have used this lovely yarn as a means of suggesting ways of arriving at similar colours by random dyeing and Navajo plying. The commercial yarn may have been space dyed but not Navajo plyed.

23m [75 ft] of 3 mm single faced satin ribbon
Pair each 3 mm (11), 3¾ (9) and 4½ mm (7) needles
3 mm (11) circular needle 60 cm long
Cable needle

MEASUREMENTS

To fit bust 92-97 cm [36-38 in.]
Length from top of shoulder 57 cm [22½ in.]
Sleeve seam 41 cm [16 in.]

TENSION

21 sts and 28 rows to 10 cm [4 in.] measured over cable patt on 4½ mm needles.

Special abbreviations
M1 – make one by picking up horizontal loop lying before next stitch and working into back of it.
C6 – cable 6 by slipping next three sts onto cable needle and leaving at front of work, K3 sts, then K3 sts from cable needle.

BACK, SLEEVES AND FRONT

Using 3¾ mm needles, cast on 78 sts and work in K1, P1 rib for 9 cm [3½ in.].
Next row Rib 3, M1 (Rib 1, M1) 5 times, (Rib 2, M1) 31 times, (Rib 1, M1) 5 times, Rib 3. [120 sts]
Change to 4½ mm needles and work in patt as follows:
1st row P2tog, yrn, P1 * K6, P1, yrn, P2tog, rep from * to end.
2nd row K3, * P6, K3, rep from * to end.
Rep 1st and 2nd rows twice more.
7th row P2tog, yrn, P1, * C6, P1, yrn, P2tog, rep from * to end.
8th row As 2nd row.
These 8 rows form patt.
Cont in patt until work measures 34 cm [13½ in.] or 7 complete patts ending on WS. (Adjust length here.)
Next row Cast on 1 st at beg of next 14 rows [134 sts], then 65 sts at beg of next 2 rows, working extra sts into patt.

FELICITY

Place a coloured thread at each end of last row. [264 sts]

Continue without shaping until work measures 17 cm [6½ in.] from coloured thread ending on wrong side.

Shape neck opening

Patt 117 sts, cast off 30 sts, patt to end.

Next row Patt to last 2 sts at neck edge, K2tog. Rejoin a separate ball of yarn to other side of neck and work both sides of neck shaping at the same time by K2tog at neck edge, patt to end.

Work 5 more rows in patt dec 1 st at both sides of neck edge.

Work 3 rows without shaping.

Work 6 rows as before but inc 1 st at both sides of neck edge.

Next row patt 117 sts, cast on 30 sts, patt to end.

Place a coloured thread at each end of last row.

Work 17 cm [6½ in.] from second coloured thread to match back.

Commence decreasing for front as follows:

Cast off 65 sts at beg of next 2 rows.   [134 sts]

Dec 1 st at beg of next 14 rows.   (120 sts]

Continue without shaping until work measures same as for back.

Dec 42 sts evenly across row.   [78 sts]

Change to 3¾ mm needles and work in K1, P1 rib for 9 cm [3½ in.]

Cast off in rib.

CUFFS (both alike)

With 3 mm needles and right side facing pick up and K49 sts evenly along edge of sleeve. K1, P1 rib for 10 cm [4 in.]. Cast off in rib.

Either

NECK BAND (plain)

With 3 mm circular needle pick up and K108 sts evenly around neck edge. Work in K1, P1 rib for 5 cm [2 in.]. Cast off in rib.

or

NECK BAND (picot cast off)

With 3 mm circular needle pick up and K108 sts evenly around neck edge.

Next round K2, * yrn, K2tog, rep from * to end. Work in K1, P1 rib for 5 cm [2 in.].

Picot cast off as follows: cast off 2 sts, * slip st left back onto left hand needle, cast on 2 sts, cast off 4 sts, rep from * to end.

TO MAKE UP

Thread ribbons through cables (making sure the colour sequence on one side is mirror reflected on the other) and sew into place on wrong side.

Sew side and sleeve seams.

Make a cord and thread through eyelet holes on picot cast off edge.

FOXGLOVES

Breed: Pick and Super
           Miscellaneous commercial
           worsted tops
Category: Shortwool and Down

The highly textured stitch pattern gives this simple slash neck sweater the designer look.

Spinning and plying instructions as for *Felicity* (page 83).

MATERIALS

Handspun – worsted tops
8 threads per cm – single ply
21 threads per in. – single ply

Commercial equivalent – double knitting (thick)
4 threads per cm
10 threads per in.

Handspun yarn
500 g space dyed worsted tops (see chapter 6)
1 pot each Dylon cold water dye shades:
A20 Radiant Pink, A3 Lilac, A11 Tahiti Rose and A19 Purple Vine random dyed

Commercial yarn
10(11) x 40 g balls Georges Picaud No. 1 Country Chiné.
Note I have used this lovely yarn as a means of suggesting ways of arriving at similar colours by space dyeing and Navajo plying. The commercial yarn may have been space dyed but was not Navajo plyed.

Pair each 4 mm (8), 4½ mm (7), 5 mm (6) and 5½ mm (5) knitting needles

MEASUREMENTS

To fit bust 81-86(91-97) cm
[32-34(36-38) in.]
Note for the larger size 91-97 cm [36-38 in.] increase needle size to 4½ mm and 5½ mm.
Length from top of shoulder 52(57) cm [20½(22½) in.]
Sleeve seam 46(51) cm [18(20) in.]

TENSION

18 sts and 23 rows to 10 cm [4 in.] over patt on 5 mm needles.

BACK AND FRONT (both alike)

With 4 mm or 4½ mm needles, cast on 65 sts and work 8 cm [3 in.] in twisted rib (knit into the back of every knit st, P1).
Change to 5 mm or 5½ mm needles and inc every 3rd st 21 times across row.   [86 sts]
P 1 row.
Now proceed in patt as follows:

CHEVRON PATTERN

Rows 1-6 Beg with P row, st st.
7th row K2, * K2tog, K3, yf, K1, yf, K3, K2tog, rep from * to last 7 sts, K2tog, K3, yf, K2.
8th row P.
9th-12th rows Rep 7th and 8th rows *twice*.
These 12 rows form patt.

FOXGLOVE PATTERN

1st row P7, * cast on 8 sts, P4, rep from * to last 3 sts, P3.
2nd row K3, * K4, P8, rep from * to last 7 sts, K7.
3rd row P7, * K8, P4, rep from * to last 3 sts, P3.
4th row K3, * K4, P8, rep from * to last 7 sts, K7.
5th row P7, * Sl1, K1, psso, K4, K2tog, P4, rep from * to last 3 sts, P3.
6th row K3, * K4, P6, rep from * to last 7 sts, K7.
7th row P7, * Sl1, K1, psso, K2, K2tog, P4, rep from * to last 3 sts, P3.
8th row K3, * K4, P4, rep from * to last 7 sts, K7.
9th row P7, * Sl1, K1, psso, K2tog, P4, rep from * to last 3 sts, P3.
10th row K3, * K4, P2, rep from * last 7 sts, K7.
11th row P7, * K2tog, P4, rep from * to last 3 sts, P3.
12th row K3, * K4, P1, rep from * to last 7 sts, K7.
13th row P7, * K2tog, P3, rep from * to last 4 sts, P4.

FOXGLOVES

14th row K.

These 14 rows form patt.

Next row P.

Rep chevron patt rows 1-12 incl.

P 1 row.

K 1 row.

Rep foxglove patt rows 1-14 incl then chevron patt rows 1-12 incl.

Next row St st 4 rows, beg with P row.

Rep foxglove patt rows 1-14 then chevron patt rows 1-12.

Next row K.

Next row P.

Change to 4 mm or 4½ mm needles and work in twisted rib for 5 cm [2 in.].

Cast off *loosely*.

SLEEVES

Using 4 mm or 4½ mm needles , cast on 45 sts and work in twisted rib for 8 cm [3 in.]

Change to 5 mm or 5½ mm needles and work inc row as follows:

K3, inc into next and every alt st across row to last 3 sts, K3. [65sts]

Next row P.

Proceed in patt as follows:

CHEVRON PATTERN

Rows 1-6 Beg with P row, st st

7th row K5, * K2tog, K3, yf, K1, yf, K3, K2tog, rep from * to last 5 sts, K5.

8th row P.

9th-12th rows Rep 7th and 8th rows *twice*.

These 12 rows form patt.

FOXGLOVE PATTERN

1st row P5, * cast on 8 sts, P4, rep from * to end.

2nd row * K4, P8, rep from * to last 5 sts, K5.

3rd row P5, * K8, P4, rep from * to end.

4th row As 2nd row.

5th row P5, * Sl1, K1, psso, K4, K2tog, P4, rep from * to end.

6th row * K4, P6, rep from * to last 5 sts, K5.

7th row P5, * Sl1, K1, psso, K2, K2tog, P4, rep from * to end.

8th row * K4, P4, rep from * to last 5 sts, K5.

9th row P5, * Sl1, K1, psso, K2tog, P4, rep from * to end.

10th row * K4, P2, rep from * to last 5 sts, K5.

11th row P5, * K2tog, P4, rep from * to end.

12th row * K4, P1, rep from * to last 5 sts, K5.

13th row P5, * K2tog, P3, rep from * to end.

14th row K.

These 14 rows form patt.

Next row P.

Next row K.

Rep chevron patt rows 1-12 incl.

P 1 row.

K 1 row.

Rep foxglove patt rows 1-14 then chevron patt rows 1-12.

Next row P.

Next row K.

Next row Rep foxglove patt rows 1-14 incl and chevron patt rows 1-12 incl.

Next row K.

Next row P.

Cast off *loosely*.

TO MAKE UP

Sew shoulder seams leaving 22 cm [8¾ in.] for neck opening.

Place centre of cast off edge of sleeve to shoulder and sew sleeves neatly into position. Join side and sleeve seams.

·10·

Knop

The lovely effect of the knop yarn is done in the plying. The core is to be spun S and the wrap Z. Both yarns are then plyed together S so the core waiting to have the knops made onto it will not disintegrate in the process.

TO SPIN

Work as per instructions on chart.

TO PLY

Holding the core in the left hand and the wrap in the right, ply at 5-7.5 cm [2-3 in.] per treadle for 4 to 6 treadles. Now make a knop by holding the core thread straight and firm and with a slow movement of the right hand, pass the wrap thread backwards and forwards over the core over approximately 1 cm [½ in.] section 4-6 times (a bit like treacle falling off a spoon! – see figs 32a, b and c) treadling once per movement and finally wrapping the wrap yarn round the whole of the knop to make a firm knot (see fig. 33). Repeat the process all over again:

1. Feed in 2-3 inches per treadle for 4-6 treadles.
2. 'Treacle' a knop and so on.

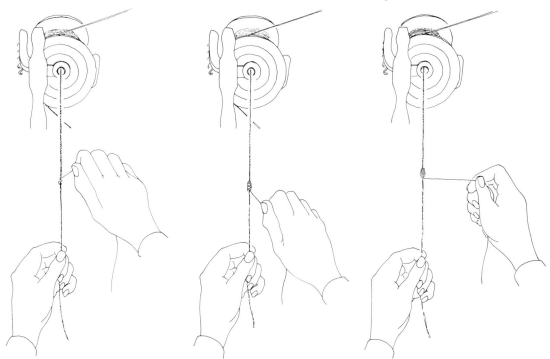

32a,b,c   *Make a knop by passing thread backwards and forwards over the core*

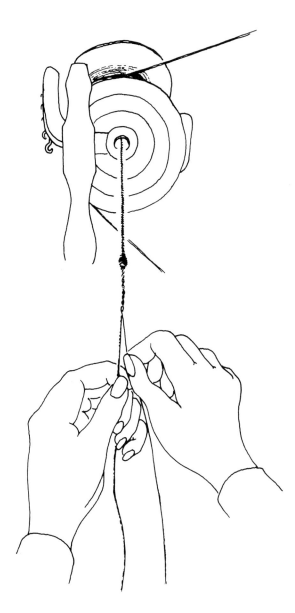

33 *Finally wrapping the wrap yarn around the whole knop to make a firm knot*

VERA

Category: Commercial worsted tops
Other fibres: Tussah Silk

A very sleek and smart side-buttoned jacket suitable for day or evening wear.

MATERIALS

Handspun – commercial worsted tops
8 threads per cm – single ply
20 threads per in. – single ply

Handspun – silk
8 threads per cm – single ply
20 threads per in. – single ply

Commercial equivalent – Aran (thin)
4.5 threads per cm
11 threads per in.

Handspun yarn
375(450:475) g brown worsted tops
75(75:75) g Tussah silk – space dyed
1 pot each Dylon cold water dye shades:
A5 Dawn Pink, A2 Sea Green, A10 Primrose
and A18 Nasturtium

Commercial yarn
10(10:11) x 50 g balls of Wendy Capri

Pair 3¾ mm (9) needles
Spare needle
11 buttons

MEASUREMENTS

To fit bust 81(86:91) cm [32(34:36) in.]
Length from shoulder 60(61:62) cm
[23½(24:24½) in.]
Sleeve seam 43(44:46) cm [17(17½:18) in.]

Knop

SPINNING INSTRUCTIONS													
Wheel Ratio	3:1	3½:1	4:1	4½:1	5:1	5½:1	6:1	6½:1	7:1	8:1	9:1	10:1	12:1
'Feed in' in inches per treadle													
Core spun S	¾	¾	1	1	1¼	1¼	1½	1¾	1¾	2	2	2½	3
Wrap spun Z	¼	¼	½	½	½-¾	¾	¾	¾	1	1	1¼	1¼	1½
PLYING INSTRUCTIONS					See plying instructions on page 95.								

VERA

TENSION

20 sts and 26 rows to 10 cm [4 in.] on 3¾ mm needles over reversed st st.

Special abbreviations

Moss st – *1st row* K1, P1 rib.

2nd row K the knit st of the previous row and P the purl st.

Rep 1st and 2nd rows throughout.

Reversed st st – right side is the purl side.

BACK

With 3¾ mm needles, cast on 88(93:98)sts and work in moss st for 5 cm [2 in.] ending with WS facing.

Still using 3¾ mm needles continue working straight in reversed st st (first row purl) until work measures 41 cm [16 in.] from cast on edge ending with WS row.

Shape armholes

Cast off 4 sts at beg next 2 rows.

Dec 1 st at beg of next 12 rows. [68(74:78)sts]

Cont straight until work measures 60(61:62) cm [23½(24:24½) in.] ending with WS row.

Shape shoulders

Cast off 7(7:9)sts at beg of next 2 rows.

Cast off 6 sts at beg of foll 2 rows.

Cast off 5(6:6)sts at beg of next 2 rows.

Cast off rem 32(36:36)sts.

LEFT FRONT

With 3¾ mm needles cast on 35(37:39)sts and work in moss st for 5 cm [2 in.].

Still using 3¾ mm needles and RS facing P to last 7 sts, moss st as set.

Next row Moss st 7 sts as set and cont to work in reversed st st as for back until work measures 41 cm [16 in.] ending with WS row.

Shape armhole

Keeping patt correct, cast off 4 sts at beg of next row.

Now dec 1 st at armhole edge on next and every foll alt row 6 times. [25(27:29)sts]

Cont straight until front measures 60(61:62) cm [23½(24:24½) in.] ending with WS row.

Shape shoulder

Keeping patt correct, cast off 6(6:8)sts at beg of next row.

Patt 1 row. [19(21:21)sts]

Rep last 2 rows once more.

Cast off 4(6:6)sts at beg of next row.

Patt 1 row.

Cast off rem sts.

RIGHT FRONT

With 3¾ mm needles cast on 75(81:87)sts and work in moss st for 2 cm [¾ in.] ending with a WS row.

Buttonhole row Moss st 4 sts, cast off next 2 sts, moss st to end.

Next row Cast on 2 sts over those cast off on previous row.

Cont in moss st as set until work measures 4 cm [1½ in.] from cast on edge, ending with a WS row.

Work the two buttonhole rows once more.

Cont in moss st until work measures 5 cm [2 in.] ending with WS row.

Next row Work the first 7 sts in moss st and the rem 68(74:80)sts in reversed st st.

Cont straight in patt as now set *at the same time* make buttonholes, as before, at 8 cm [3¼ in.] intervals from last buttonhole until front measures 41 cm [16 in.] from cast on edge.

Shape armhole

Keeping patt correct and still working buttonholes cast off 4 sts at beg of next row.

Patt 1 row.

Dec 1 st at beg of next and every foll alt row 6 times. [65(71:77)sts]

Cont straight until front measures 54(55:56) cm [21¼(21¾:22) in.] ending at neck edge.

Shape neck

Patt across the first 23(25:27)sts, turn and leave rem 42(46:50)sts on a spare needle.

Dec 1 st at neck edge on every row 4 times in all, then dec 1 st on every foll alt row twice in all. [17(19:21)sts]

Work straight until front measures 59(60:61) cm [23¼(23½:24) in.] from cast on edge, ending WS.

Next row Place moss sts on a spare needle. Cast off next 4(4:6)sts. Work to end.

Work 1 row.

Cast off rem 6(8:8)sts.

With RS facing return to rem sts and cast off 16(18:20)sts at centre front, patt to end.

Dec 1 st at neck edge on every row 4 times in all, then dec 1 st on every foll alt row 3 times in all. [19(21:23)sts]

Cont on these sts until front measures 60(61:62) cm [23½(24:24½) in.] from cast on edge, ending WS.

Shape shoulder

Cast off 6(6:8)sts at beg of next row.

Patt 1 row.

Cast off 8 sts at beg of foll row.

Patt 1 row.

Cast off rem 7(9:9)sts.

SLEEVES

With 3¾ mm needles cast on 45(47:49)sts and work in moss st for 6 cm [2½ in.].

Still using 3¾ mm needles work in reversed st st inc 1 st at each end of the next and every foll 6th row until there are 67(71:75)sts. Cont straight until work measures 43(44:46) cm [17(17½:18) in.] from beg ending WS.

Shape top

Cast off 4 sts at beg of next 2 rows.

Now dec 1 st at beg of next 29(33:35) rows. [30(30:32)sts]

Dec 1 st at each end of every row for next 10 rows.

Cast off rem 10(10:12)sts.

Neck band

Sew right shoulder seams and with right side facing and 3¾ mm needles pick up and knit 18 sts down left front, 16(18:20)sts across centre front, 18 sts up right front and 32(36:36)sts from back neck. [84(90:92)sts]

Work in moss st for 3 cm [1¼ in.]. Cast off in moss st.

Now moss st across the held 7 sts on safety pin. Pick up and knit 7(9:9)sts across leftfront shoulder and 6 sts across neck band. [20(22:22)sts]

Work in moss st for 2 cm [¾ in.] ending with WS.

Buttonhole row Moss st 4 sts, cast off 2 sts, moss st 3(4:4)sts, cast off 2 sts, moss st 3(4:4)sts, cast off 2 sts, moss st 4 sts. (3 buttonholes made across shoulder.)

Next row Cast on 2 sts over those cast off on the previous row.

Cast off in moss st.

TO MAKE UP

Sew left front shoulder to back seam.

Set in sleeves.

Join side seams.

Sew on buttons to correspond with buttonholes.

FLORENCE

FLORENCE

Category: Commercial worsted tops
Other fibre: Silk

Square-neck sweater with set in sleeves knitted in garter stitch and stocking stitch throughout – simple but smart. (See page 96 for spinning and plying instructions.)

MATERIALS

Handspun – commercial worsted tops
8 threads per cm – single ply
20 threads per in. – single ply

Handspun – silk
8 threads per cm – single ply
20 threads per in. – single ply

Commercial equivalent – Aran (thin)
4.5 threads per cm
11 threads per in.

Handspun yarn
225(225:225:225) g white worsted tops
25(25:25:25) g blue worsted tops
} blended together
150(150:200:200) g cultivated silk

Commercial yarn
8(8:9:9) x 50 g balls of Wendy Capri

Pair each 3¼ mm (10) and 3¾ mm (9) needles

MEASUREMENTS

To fit bust 81(86:91:97) cm [32(34:36:38) in.]
Length from shoulder 50(50.5:52:52.5) cm [19½(19¾:20½:20¾) in.]
Sleeve seam 42.5 cm [16¾) in.]

TENSION

22 sts and 28 rows to 10 cm [4 in.] on 3¾ mm needles over st st.

BACK

With 3¼ mm needles cast on 83(89:95:101)sts and work 23 rows in garter st (every row knit).
Inc row Inc 11 sts evenly across row.

[94(100:106:112)sts]
Change to 3¾ mm needles and st st 76 rows ending WS. **

Shape armholes
Cast off 4 sts at beg next 2 rows, then dec 1 st at each end of the next 6(7:9:10) rows.
[74(78:80:84)sts]
St st 31(31:34:34) rows.

Shape neck
Work 19(21:22:24)sts, leave these on a safety pin for right back shoulder, cast off 36 sts, work to end. Work on these 19(21:22:24)sts. Dec 1 st at neck edge on each of the next 8 rows.
[11(13:14:16)sts]
(*Note* work 1 row extra here when working left back shoulder.)

Shape shoulders
Cast off 4(5:5:5)sts at beg of next row and 4(5:5:5)sts at beg of foll alt row. Work 1 row. Cast off rem 3(3:4:6)sts.

Left back shoulder
(RS) Rejoin yarn to neck edge and work as given for right back shoulder, working extra row, where indicated.

FRONT

Work as for back to **.

Shape armhole
Cast off 4 sts at beg of next row.

Shape armhole and divide for neck
Cast off 4 sts. P a further 17(20:23:36)sts and leave these 18(21:24:27)sts on a safety pin. Cast off next 50 sts. P to end.
Work on these 18(21:24:27)sts for left half front.
Cont armhole shaping by keeping neck edge straight and dec 1 st at armhole edge on the next 6(7:9:10) rows.   [12(14:15:17)sts]
St st 40(40:43:43) rows, dec 1 st at armhole edge on last row.
(*Note* when working right half front work one extra row.)

Shape shoulder
Cast off 4(5:5:5)sts at beg of next row and 4(5:5:5)sts at beg of foll alt row.
Work 1 row. Cast off rem 3(3:4:6)sts.

Right half front

(RS) Rejoin yarn to neck edge and work as given for left half front, working extra row where indicated.

SLEEVES

With 3¼ mm needles cast on 44(48:50:50)sts and work 23 rows in garter st.
Change to 3¾ mm needles and working in st st inc 1 st at each end of the next and every foll 8th row until there are 66(70:72:76)sts.
Work straight for a further 19 rows.

Sleeve top

Cast off 4 sts at beg of next 2 rows.
Dec 1 st at each end of next and the foll 15 alt rows.   [28(32:34:38)sts]
Purl 1 row.
Dec 1 st at each end of the next 6(8:9:10) rows.
Cast off rem 16 sts.

NECK BAND

Using   3¼ mm   needles   cast   on 198(198:204:204)sts
1st row K42(42:45:45), K3tog, K49, K3tog, K101(101:105:105).
2nd and every alt row K.
3rd row K41(41:44:44), K3tog, K47, K3tog, K to end.

5th row K40(40:43:43), K3tog, K45, K3tog, K to end.
7th row K39(39:42:42), K3tog, K43, K3tog, K to end.
9th row K38(38:41:41), K3tog, K41, K3tog, K to end.
11th row K37(37:40:40), K3tog, K39, K3tog, K37(37:40:40), (K2, K2tog) 5 times, K10 (K2tog, K2) to end.   [162(162:168:168)sts]
13th row K36(36:39:39), K3tog, K37, K3tog, K to end.
15th row K35(35:38:38), K3tog, K35, K3tog, K to end.
17th row K34(34:37:37), K3tog, K33, K3tog, K to end.
19th row K33(33:36:36), K3tog, K31, K3tog, K to end.
21st row K32(32:35:35), K3tog, K29, K3tog, K32(32:35:35), (K1, K2tog) 5 times, (K2tog, K1) to end.   [125(125:132:132)sts]
Work 1 row.
Cast off.

TO MAKE UP

Join shoulder seams and set in sleeves.
Join side and sleeve seams.
Beginning at left shoulder sew cast on edge of neck band all round neck edging.

·11·

Bouclé

It does seem a lot of work and effort to produce bouclé but nevertheless it is *very* worth while. Almost any fibres worked together will produce this yarn and so ideas are endless. Wool on wool is lovely and easy to bouclé but the cotton on the wool and mohair blend gives a cooler alternative to the yarn and although cultivated silk is a little more expensive, it does give a wonderful sheen.

However, using silk as the yarn to bouclé over the wool is a little more difficult. It is important to have a friction-free lazy kate for smooth flow and to have the silk on the lazy kate *below* the wool. Dampening the finger and thumb of the right hand, which is pushing the silk into the bouclé, makes it much easier to handle.

TO SPIN

Follow the chart instructions, noting carefully the direction of S or Z of the yarn to be spun.

It is a useful tip to mark each bobbin A, B or C for easy identification.

TO PLY

First ply – Z

Work near the orifice and treadle *slowly*.

A jumbo attachment or large cup hooks on the flyer will be necessary for this yarn.

The lazy kate is on the floor immediately under the orifice.

Hold the core A in the left hand and the loop B in the right (see fig. 34). Feed in both strands together at approximately 5-7.5 cm [2-3 in.] per treadle for three treadles. Now make the bouclé by holding the core thread straight and firm and with a slow movement of the right hand with the thumb and finger push the loop threads up the core thread to form small wrinkled lumps (bunches – see fig. 35). Wait until the twist catches these bunches, feed onto the bobbin and repeat the process. It is important to work this yarn to an even rhythm as any delay in making the bouclé bunches will result in the core threads being held back and creating a strain, possibly resulting in disintegration.

Second ply – S

Hold the first plyed core or loop threads in the left hand and the wrap C in the right, but working much closer together than in the first ply. Feed in evenly and regularly letting the bouclé yarn wrap around the wrap yarn in the right hand (see fig. 36). *At the same time* with the left finger and thumb tidy up the bunches (see fig. 37) before they are finally plyed together as they pass through these fingers ready to be wrapped.

By holding the yarn in separate hands, the eyes have a clear view to see if the yarn coming up to be plyed will need tidying.

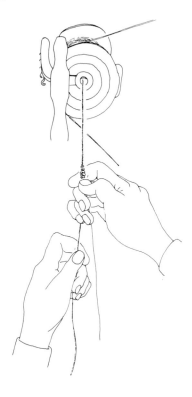

34 *Hold core A in left hand and loop B in right hand*

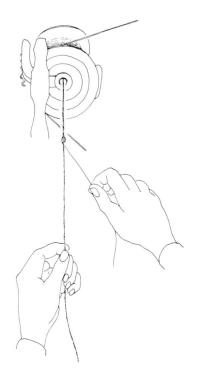

35 *Make the bouclé by holding the core thread straight and with finger and thumb of right hand push loop threads up core to form a small wrinkled bunch*

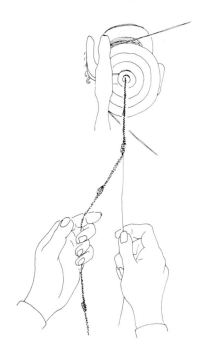

36 *Second ply S – let first core or loop wrap the wrap . . .*

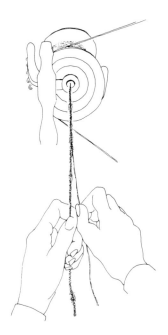

37 *. . . at the same time with left hand tidy up the lumps before finally plying*

▨▨ PAPILLON ▨▨

Breed: Shetland
Category: Shortwool and Down
Other fibres: Mohair (goat)
                Cotton

It is the lovely butterfly stitch in this slash-neck sweater that makes it so exciting to knit.

MATERIALS

Handspun – two types of yarn
Main – 100 per cent cotton
10 threads per cm – single ply
25 threads per in. – single ply
Contrast – wool/mohair blend with cotton
(See bouclé instructions on page 103.)

Commercial equivalent

Main – 100 per cent cotton double knitting (thin)
5.5 threads per cm
14 threads per in.
Contrast – wool/mohair/cotton Aran (thin)
4.5 threads per cm
11 threads per in.

Handspun yarn

350 g cotton for the main yarn
400 g cotton for the bouclé yarn *with*
200 g wool and
200 g mohair   blended together

Commercial yarn

Main – 5 x 50 g balls Georges Picaud Akala
Contrast – 7 x 50 g balls Georges Picaud Fifi.

Pair each 4 mm (8) and 5 mm (6) needles

MEASUREMENTS

To fit bust 86(91) cm [34(36) in.]
Length from top of shoulder 53 cm [21 in.]
Sleeve seam 49 cm [19 in.]

TENSION

16 sts and 25 rows to 10 cm [4 in.] measured over pattern on 5 mm needles.

Special abbreviations

Pick-up stitch for butterfly pattern is done by working the next stitch knitwise, taking up *at the same time* the 4 threads stretched in front of the slip stitches.
M – main; C – contrast

BACK AND FRONT (both alike)

Using M and 4 mm needles, cast on 60 sts and work 8 cm [3 in.] in K1, P1 rib by working two rows in M, and two rows in C, ending with two rows in M.
Next row In C increase 17 sts evenly across row. [77 sts]
Next row P.
Change to 5 mm needles and proceed in patt as follows:
1st to 6th row In M, K.
7th, 9th, 11th and 13th rows In C, K.
8th, 10th, 12th and 14th rows In C, K1 * leaving yarn in knit position, Sl5 purlwise, K5 * rep from * to last 6 sts, Sl5 purlwise, K1.
15th row K3, * pick-up stitch, K9, rep from * to last 4 sts, pick-up st, K3.
16th row In C, P.
17th-22nd rows In M, K.

Bouclé for Papillon and Una

SPINNING INSTRUCTIONS													
Wheel Ratio	3:1	3½:1	4:1	4½:1	5:1	5½:1	6:1	6½:1	7:1	8:1	9:1	10:1	12:1
'Feed in' in inches per treadle													
Core spun Z					½-¾	¾	¾	¾	1	1	1¼	1¼	1½
Loop spun S					½-¾	¾	¾	¾	1	1	1¼	1¼	1½
Wrap spun Z					½-¾	¾	¾	¾	1	1	1¼	1¼	1½
PLYING INSTRUCTIONS				See plying instructions on page 103.									

PAPILLON

23rd, 25th, 27th and 29th rows In C, K.
24th, 26th, 28th and 30th rows In C, K6, leaving yarn in knit position Sl5 purlwise, K5, rep from * to last 11 sts, Sl5 purlwise, K6.
31st row K8, * pick-up stitch, K9, rep from * to last 8 sts, K8.
32nd row In C, P.
These 32 rows form patt.
Work 2 more complete patterns and then rows 1-22. (50 cm [19½ in.])
Change to 4 mm needles and beg with C work 5 cm [2 in.] in K1, P1 rib alternating every two rows as before with M and C.
Cast off in M.

SLEEVES

Using 4 mm needles and M, cast on 30 sts and K1, P1 rib for 8 cm [3 in.] working two rows in M and two rows in C, ending with M.
Next row In C, K increasing 27 sts evenly across row. [57 sts]
Next row P.
Change to 5 mm needles and proceed in patt as for back working three complete patterns and then rows 1-22. (49 cm [19 in.])
Cast off in M.

TO MAKE UP

Sew shoulder seams.
Leave 22 cm [8¾ in.] for neck opening.
Place centre of cast off edge of sleeve to shoulder and sew neatly into position down side edge.
Join side and sleeve seams.

UNA

Breed:　　　Shetland
Category:　　Shortwool and Down
Other fibres:　Mohair (goat)
　　　　　　　Cotton

The use of partial knitting as in this sweater is an excellent way of enhancing different texture yarns by moving across with a thick yarn and moving into thin (remembering to balance on the other side at a later stage by reversing the thickness and thinness of yarns). (See page 105 for spinning and plying instructions.)

MATERIALS

Handspun – two types of yarn
Main – 100 per cent cotton
10 threads per cm – single ply
25 threads per in. – single ply
Contrast – wool/mohair blend with cotton
(See bouclé instructions on page 103.)

Commercial equivalent
Main – 100 per cent cotton double knitting (thin)
5.5 threads per cm
14 threads per in.
Contrast – wool/mohair/cotton Aran (thin)
4.5 threads per cm
11 threads per in.

Handspun yarn
500 g cotton for the main yarn
250 g cotton for the bouclé yarn *with*
150 g wool and
150 g mohair　} blended together

Commercial yarn
Main – 7 x 50 g balls Georges Picaud Akala
Contrast – 5 x 50 g balls Georges Picaud Fifi.

Pair each 4 mm (8) and 5 mm (6) needles

MEASUREMENTS

To fit bust 86(91) cm [34(36) in.]
Length from top of shoulder 53 cm [21 in.]
Sleeve seam 49 cm [19 in.]

TENSION

16 sts and 25 rows to 10 cm [4 in.] measured over pattern on 5 mm needles.

Special abbreviations
M – main; C – contrast

BACK AND FRONT (both alike)

With M and 4 mm needles, cast on 60 sts and work 8 cm [3 in.] in K1, P1 rib working two rows with M and two rows with C, ending with two rows in M.
Next row In C, K, inc into every 4th st. [74 sts]

UNA

Next row In C, P.

Change to 5 mm needles and in M, K 5 rows.

Now work in partial knitting patt as follows:

1st row In C, P.

2nd row K.

3rd and 4th rows P50, turn, slip next st, K to end.

5th and 6th rows P25, turn, slip next st, K to end.

7th row In M, P.

8th–11th rows K.

12th row In C, K.

13th row P.

14th and 15th rows K50, turn, Sl next st, P to end.

16th and 17th rows K25, turn, Sl next st, P to end.

18th–22nd rows In M, K.

These 22 rows form patt.

Cont in patt until 5 complete patts have been worked (49 cm[19½ in.]) ending with 21st row.

Change to 4 mm needles and beginning with C, rib K1, P1 for 5 cm [2 in.] alternating every two rows as before with M and C.

Cast off in M.

SLEEVES

With M and 4 mm needles, cast on 30 sts and rib K1, P1 for 8 cm [3 in.] working two rows with M and two rows with C as for back, ending with M.

Next row Change to C and using 5 mm needles P 1 row.

Next row Knit, inc into every st. [60 sts]

Next row P.

Change to M and knit 5 rows.

Commence partial knitting patt as follows:

1st row In C, P.

2nd row K.

3rd and 4th rows P40, turn, sl next st, K to end.

5th and 6th rows P20, turn, sl next st, K to end.

7th row In M, P.

8th–11th rows K.

12th row In C, K.

13th row P.

14th and 15th rows K40, turn, Sl next st, P to end.

16th and 17th rows K20, turn, Sl next st, P to end.

18th–22nd rows In M, K.

These 22 rows form patt.

Cont in patt until 5 complete patts have been worked, ending with 21st row. (49 cm [19 in.])

Cast off in M.

TO MAKE UP

Sew shoulder seams leaving 22 cm [8¾ in.] for neck opening.

Place centre of cast off edge of sleeve to shoulder seams and sew sleeves neatly into position.

Join side and sleeve seams.

·12·

Curled loop

Although the thicknesses of the yarns and the spinning instructions are different from bouclé, the procedure is very similar with one or two exceptions:

1. The fleece *must* be long stapled and preferably lustrous; a short staple fleece will only bouclé and not loop.
2. The looping is repeated on each treadle producing a completed yarn of continuous loops.

The hands will move 2 to 3 inches apart but by the time the loops are pushed up and made, the gap between the previous loop and the new one has practically closed.

TO SPIN

Follow the chart instructions, noting carefully the direction of S or Z of the yarn to be spun.

It is a useful tip to mark each bobbin A, B or C for easy identification.

FIRST PLY – S

Work near the orifice and treadle *slowly*.

A jumbo attachment or large cup hooks on the flyer will be necessary for this yarn.

The lazy kate is on the floor immediately under the orifice.

Hold the core in the right hand and the loop B in the left.

Bring strands together and make loop by sliding the left hand finger and thumb up the core A thread taking the loop B thread with it, wait until the twist catches hold of the loops and then feed onto the bobbin. Now part hands again and take a fresh hold on the two yarns 2 or 3 inches further back, ready for the next treadle and repeat the loop process (see fig. 35).

This process is carried out every treadle.

As loop B is slid along the core A, because of the length of staple of the fleece the loops are formed very easily.

If treadling is too quick, the yarns will ply normally and there will not be sufficient play in the yarns to permit looping.

SECOND PLY – Z

Hold the first plyed core or loop threads in the left hand and the wrap C in the right, but working much closer together than in the first ply. Feed in evenly and regularly letting the loop yarn wrap around the wrap yarn in right hand. *At the same time* with the left hand finger and thumb tidy up the loops by spacing them evenly apart before they are finally plyed together as they pass through the fingers to be wrapped (see fig. 37). By holding the yarn in separate hands, you will be able to see clearly if the yarn coming up to be plyed will need tidying.

This is a very easy and attractive yarn to create and will allow you to interchange colours and make many beautiful garments.

▰▰▰▰ ALETHEA ▰▰▰▰

Breed: Wensleydale
Category: Longwool and Lustre
Other fibres: Coloured lustre worsted tops

Curled loop sweater with Spanish lace panel.

MATERIALS

Handspun – for the bouclé yarn
A – double knitting (thin) for the core spun Z
10 threads per cm – single ply
25 threads per in. – single ply
B – Aran (thin) for the loop spun Z
8 threads per cm – single ply
20 threads per in. – single ply
C – double knitting (thin) for the wrap spun S
10 threads per cm – single ply
25 threads per in. – single ply

Commercial equivalent – chunky
3 threads per cm
7/8 threads per in.

Handspun – for the panel pattern and welts.
10 threads per cm – single ply
25 threads per in. – single ply

Commercial equivalent – double knitting (thin)
5.5 threads per cm
14 threads per in.

Handspun yarn – for the bouclé
250(300:350) g Wensleydale (essential to use Longwool and Lustre fleece)
250(300:300) g lilac coloured lustre worsted tops (or dyed Wensleydale)
These two are very casually blended together to give a prominent two-tone effect

400(400:500) g plum coloured worsted tops for the core and wrap

Handspun yarn – for the panel pattern and welts
300(350:350) g plum coloured worsted tops

Commercial yarn
16(18:20) x 50 g balls Emu Florentine
6(6:7) x 50 g balls Superwash Double Knitting.

Pair each 5 mm (6) and 7 mm (2) needles

MEASUREMENTS

To fit bust 91(97:102) cm [36(38:40) in.]
Length from top of shoulder 58 cm [23 in.]
Sleeve seam 43 cm [17 in.]

TENSION

16 sts and 16 rows to 10 cm [4 in.] measured over pattern on 7 mm needles.

SPECIAL INSTRUCTIONS

Do not take curled loop or Florentine yarn across the panel pattern stitches. Use two separate balls of the curled loop yarn, one for each side of the panel and twist the double knitting yarn at beginning of each section to avoid a hole in work.

SPECIAL ABBREVIATIONS

B – bouclé yarn; C – contrast yarn

SPANISH LACE PATTERN (34 stitches)

1st row K3, K2tog, K4, M1, P2, (K2, wrn, Sl1, K1, psso) 3 times, P2, M1, K4, Sl1, K1, psso, K3.

Curled loop

SPINNING INSTRUCTIONS													
Wheel Ratio	3:1	3½:1	4:1	4½:1	5:1	5½:1	6:1	6½:1	7:1	8:1	9:1	10:1	12:1
'Feed in' in inches per treadle													
Core spun Z					½-¾	¾	¾	¾	1	1	1¼	1¼	1½
Loop spun Z	¾	¾	1	1	1¼	1½	1½	1¾	1¾	2	2	2½	3
Wrap spun S	1	1¼	1¼	1½	1¾	1¾	2	2¼	2½	2½	3	3¼	4
PLYING INSTRUCTIONS				See plying instructions on page 111.									

ALETHEA

2nd row P2, P2tog, tbl, P4, M1, P1, K2, (P2, M1, P2tog) 3 times, K2, P1, M1, P4, P2tog, P2.

3rd row K1, K2tog, K4, M1, K2, P2, (K2, M1, Sl1, K1, psso) 3 times, P2, K2, M1, K4, Sl1, K1, psso, K1.

4th row P2tog, tbl, P4, M1, P3, K2, (P2, M1, P2tog) 3 times, K2, P3, M1, P4, P2tog.

Repeat rows 1-4 twice more.

13th row M1, Sl1, K1, psso, K2, M1, Sl1, K1, psso, P2, M1, K4, Sl1, K1, psso, K6, K2tog, K4, M1, P2, K2, M1, Sl1, K1, psso, K2.

14th row M1, P2tog, P2, M1, P2tog, K2, P1, M1, P4, P2tog, P4, P2tog, tbl, P4, M1, P1, K2, P2, M1, P2tog, P2.

15th row M1, Sl1, K1, psso, K2, M1, Sl1, K1, psso, P2, K2, M1, K4, Sl1, K1, psso, K2, K2tog, K4, M1, K2, P2, K2, M1, Sl1, K1, psso, K2.

16th row M1, P2tog, P2, M1, P2tog, K2, P3, M1, P4, P2tog, P2tog, tbl, P4, M1, P3, K2, P2, M1, P2tog, P2.

Repeat rows 13-16 twice more.

These 24 rows form panel pattern.

BACK AND FRONT (both alike)

With 5 mm needles and C, cast on 64(68:72)sts and work in K1, P1 rib for 7 cm [3 in.].

Change to 7 mm needles and B, K15(19:23)sts. Change to C and work 1st row of panel pattern to last 15(19:23)sts. Change to B, and K these sts.

Next row With B, P15(19:23)sts. Change to C and work panel patt 2nd row.

Change to B. P to end.

Cont in yarns as set working each side of the panel patt in B and the centre panel in C until work measures 36 cm [14 in.]. Place a coloured marker thread at each end of work to mark sleeve position.

Cont as before until work measures 18 cm [7 in.] from sleeve markers. (3 complete panel patts from beg)

Change to C and 5 mm needles and work in K1, P1 rib for 5 cm [2 in.]. Cast off *loosely* in rib.

SLEEVES

With C and 5 mm needles, cast on 28(30:32)sts.

Work in K1, P1 rib for 8 cm [3 in.], inc 20(20:24)sts evenly across last row. [48(50:56)sts]

Change to 7 mm needles and B and work in st st inc 1 st at each end of next and every foll 4th row until there are 68(68:72)sts.

Cont without shaping until work measures 43 cm [17 in.].

Cast off *loosely*.

TO MAKE UP

Sew shoulder seams leaving 22 cm [8½ in.] gap for neck opening.

Fold sleeves in half, place fold on shoulder seam and set between the two markers.

Sew side and sleeve seams.

·13·
Crepe-double knitting and chunky

DOUBLE KNITTING

Crepe is a very popular yarn for most commercial spinners, and when it has been handspun it is easy to see why. It has a lovely feel spun either thick or thin with the strands folding in neatly together.

Surprisingly the easiest way of bringing out the best in the plys is to have three bobbins of the same shade and one bobbin multi-coloured. Two bobbins of the same shade are plyed together S, and the other two bobbins (one a multi-coloured shade and the other the same shade as bobbins one and two) are plyed together, again S.

Lastly the two resulting bobbins, making all four strands, come together and are plyed Z. The multi-coloured strand neatly interlaces into the other three plys, and the result is very attractive indeed.

▰▰▰ DANIELLE ▰▰▰

Breed: Shetland
Category: Shortwool and Down

A stunning shawl neck sweater in campanula stitch with knitted shoulder pads.

MATERIALS

Handspun
18 threads per cm – single ply
45 threads per in. – single ply
4 bobbins plyed together – see Spinning and Plying Chart on page 115

Commercial equivalent – double knitting (thin)
5.5 threads per cm
14 threads per in.

Crepe DK

SPINNING INSTRUCTIONS													
Wheel Ratio	3:1	3½:1	4:1	4½:1	5:1	5½:1	6:1	6½:1	7:1	8:1	9:1	10:1	12:1
'Feed in' in inches per treadle spun Z	½-¾	¾	¾	¾	1	1	1¼	1¼	1½	1½	1¾	2	2½

PLYING INSTRUCTIONS													
Ply the four bobbins in two sets of two S Per treadles per 18 inches	15	12	12	12	9	9	8	8	6	6	5	4½	3½
Ply the two resulting bobbins Z	8	7	7	7	5	5	5	5	4	4	3½	3½	2¾

DANIELLE

Handspun yarn

700(700:800) g Shetland (either dyed or plain)
200(200:200) g Shetland random or space dyed
multi-coloured.

Commercial yarn

10(10:11) x 50 g balls Sirdar Country Style
Tweed Double Crepe

Pair each 3¼ mm (10) and 4 mm (8) needles
Circular needle 3¼ mm (10) 60 cm long

MEASUREMENTS

To fit bust 87(90:97) cm [34(36:38) in.]
Length from top of shoulder 66(67:68) cm
[26(26½:27) in.]
Sleeve seam 44 cm [17¼ in.]

TENSION

24 sts and 28 rows to 10 cm [4 in.] over patt on
4 mm needles.

Special instructions

The circular needle is used for completing the
collar. *Do not use it in rounds*, but work
backwards and forwards in the usual way.

BACK

With 3¼ mm needles cast on 97(103:109)sts
and work in K1, P1 rib for 8 cm [3 in.].
Inc row Inc 21(20:19)sts evenly across row.
[118(123:128)sts]
Change to 4 mm needles and work in patt as
follows:
1st row K1, * K3, P2, rep, from * to last st, K1.
2nd and alt rows K1, * K2, P3, rep from * to last
st, K1.
3rd row As 1st row.
5th row K1, * yrn, Sl1, K2tog, psso, M1, P2,
rep from * to last st, K1.
These 6 rows form patt.
Cont straight in patt until back measures 44 cm
[14½ in.] ending WS.

Shape armholes

Keeping patt correct, cast off 4 sts at beg of next
4 rows.
Dec 1 st at each end of next 5(7:9) rows by K1,
K2tog, patt to last 3 sts, Sl1, K1, psso, K1. **
Work 1 row.

Dec 1 st at each of next and 2 foll alt rows as
before.[86(87:90)sts].
Cont straight until armhole measures
22(23:24) cm [8½(9:9½) in.] ending WS.

Shape shoulders

Cast off 11 sts at beg of next 4 rows. Leave rem
42(43:46)sts on a stitch holder.

FRONT

Work as for back to **.
Work 1 row.

Shape front neck

With RS facing, dec 1 st, patt 42(43:44)sts, K2
tog, *turn*. Leave rem 46(46:48)sts on spare
needle.
Work 1 row.
*** Dec 1 st each end of next and foll alt row.
Cont straight at armhole edge *but* cont to dec on
every alt row at neck edge until 22 sts rem.
Work straight until front measures the same as
back to shoulder shaping ending at armhole
edge.

Shape shoulders

Cast off 11 sts at beg of next and foll alt row.
With RS facing, rejoin yarn to sts on spare
needle. Patt to last 2 sts, K2tog.
Work 1 row.
Now work as for first side from *** to end.

SLEEVES

With 3¼ mm needles, cast on 55(57:59)sts and
work in K1, P1 rib for 8 cm [3 in.].
Inc row Inc 55(55:58)sts evenly across row.
[107(112:117)sts]
Change to 4 mm needles and work straight in
campanula st patt as for back until work
measures 44 cm [17½ in.] ending WS.

Shape top

Keeping patt correct, cast off 4 sts at beg of next
4 rows.
Dec 1 st at each end of next and every foll alt
row until 53(52:53)sts remain.
Cast off 4 sts at beg of next 6 rows. Cast off rem
sts.

COLLAR

Join both shoulder seams.

With 3¼ mm circular needle, beg at the first dec st at right centre front, pick up and K52 sts evenly along edge of shoulder seam, K42(43:46)sts from back neck, then pick up and K51 sts evenly down left neck edge. [145(146:149)sts]

Work in K1, P1 rib for 14 cm [5½ in.]. Cast off in rib.

SHOULDER PADS (make 2)

With 3¼ mm needles cast on 37 sts. Work 43 rows in K1, P1 rib.

Cast off in rib.

TO MAKE UP

Join side and sleeve seams. Set in sleeves.

Stitch collar into place at front.

Fold shoulder pads into triangles and sew round edge.

Sew into sweater.

CHUNKY

Crepe chunky follows the same procedure as for crepe double knitting, except that the threads per inch will be fewer and slightly different in plying.

Two bobbins of the same shade (white) are plyed together S, and the other two bobbins (peach and lemon) are plyed together S but at only 6 treadles per 18 inches. Lastly, the two resulting bobbins, making the four strands come together, are plyed Z but this time only a mere 1½ treadles per 18 inches, giving a lovely soft-to-handle yarn that is *very* quick to knit.

Putting the two white strands together and then the two coloured strands together, instead of one plain and one coloured on each, keeps the yarn soft looking and not busy as would have been the case if separated.

ETHEL

Breed: Shetland worsted tops
Category: Shortwool and Down
Other fibres: Samoyed dog hair and mohair
               (goat)

A lovely soft quick-to-knit bolero, ideal for wearing on any occasion.

MATERIALS

Handspun

4 separate bobbins each spun at
8 threads per cm – single ply
20 threads per in. – single ply

Commercial equivalent – chunky
3 threads per cm
7/8 threads per in.

Handspun yarn

150 g deep orange dog hair (or mohair) } blended together
50 g white Shetland worsted tops } to make peach

150 g deep yellow Samoyed dog hair (or mohair) } blended together
50 g white Shetland worsted tops } to make lemon

250 g mohair white } blended together
150 g Shetland worsted tops }

1 pot each Dylon cold water dye shades:
A27 Mandarin and A22 Sahara Sun

Commercial yarn

8(9) x 100 g balls Emu Snowball
Note this yarn is the same thickness as the handspun chunky crepe but it is *not* a crepe yarn.

Pair each 7 mm (2) and 8 mm (0) needles

MEASUREMENTS

To fit bust 81-87(92-97) cm
[32-34(36-38) in.]
Length from top of shoulder 47(51) cm
[18½(20) in.]

TENSION

10 sts and 14 rows to 10 cm [4 in.] over st st on 8 mm needles.

Crepe chunky

SPINNING INSTRUCTIONS

Wheel Ratio	3:1	3½:1	4:1	4½:1	5:1	5½:1	6:1	6½:1	7:1	8:1	9:1	10:1	12:1
'Feed in' in inches per treadle Z	½	¾	¾	¾	1	1	1¼	1¼	1½	1½	1¾	2	2½

PLYING INSTRUCTIONS

Ply the four bobbins in two sets of two S
Per treadles per 18 inches   6
Ply the two resultings bobbins Z
Per treadles per 18 inches   1½

119

ETHEL

BACK

With 7 mm needles cast on 42(48)sts and work in K1, P1 rib for 2.5 cm [1 in.].
Change to 8 mm needles and work in st st until back measures 25(27) cm [10(10½) in.].

Shape armholes

Cast off 2 sts at beg of next 2 rows.
Cast off 1 st at beg of foll 2 rows.
Dec 1 st at each end of next 2 rows. [32(38)sts]
Cont straight until armhole measures 20(23) cm [8(9) in.].

Shape shoulders

With RS facing cast off 3(4)sts at beg of next 3 rows.
Cast off 4 sts at beg of next 2 rows.
Cast off 3(4)sts at beg of next row. Cast off rem 12(14)sts.

RIGHT FRONT

With 8 mm needles cast on 14(16)sts and st st 6 rows, inc 1 st at centre of work on each row. [20(22)sts]
Cont straight in st st until front measures 15(16.5) cm [6(6½) in.] ending at front edge.
Dec 1 st at front edge on next and every alt row until 16 sts rem.
Cont straight until work measures 22(24) cm [8½(9½) in.] ending at side edge.

Shape armhole

Cast off 2 sts at beg of next row, then cast off 1 st at beg of foll alt row.
Dec 1 st at armhole edge on next 2 rows.
Cont straight in st st until armhole measures 20(23) cm [8(9) in.] ending armhole edge.

Shape shoulder

Cast off 3(4)sts at beg of next and foll alt row.
Work 1 row.
Cast off rem 3 sts.

LEFT FRONT

Work as for right front but reversing all shapings.

ARMBANDS (both alike)

Join shoulder seams.
With 7 mm needles and RS facing pick up and K48(52)sts.
Work in K1, P1 rib for 3 cm [1¼ in.].
Cast off in rib.

FRONT BAND

With 7 mm needles, cast on 7 sts and work in rib as follows:
1st row K2, (P1, K1) twice, P1.
2nd row K1, (P1, K1) twice, P1, K1.
Rep these 2 rows until band fits when slightly stretched from one side seam to beg of lower front shaping.   [16 rows]
Cont as follows:
1st row Rib 4 sts, as set, turn.
2nd row Sl1, rib to end.
3rd and 4th rows Rib to end.
Rep these 4 rows 3 times until band fits around curve of lower front.
Now work 10(12) cm [4½(4¾) in.] straight in rib.
Next row Inc 1 st at inside edge of band on next and every foll alt row until there are 13(15)sts on needle.
Cont straight in rib until band reaches centre back of neck.
Mark this point. Continue working other half of band to match.

TO MAKE UP

Join bands to fronts and back of bolero.
Join side and armband seams.

Marl

To make a good marl yarn, drum carding of all fibres is an asset. However, it is necessary to work in rovings.

TO PREPARE

Make separate rovings of *two* separate colours (this is where the drum carded batts would be of help). If rolags are used, first draw them out into rovings and then lay the two separate colours side by side and redraw them out to near the correct thickness for spinning, letting the continuous roving fall softly into a plastic bucket in order to disturb the fibres as little as possible.

This two-tone yarn is then plyed with a third tone which will produce a tweed yarn.

See chart on page 000 for spinning and plying instructions.

ZOE

Category: Commercially coloured worsted tops
Some Longwool and Lustre

Bold vivid colours come together in this diametric sweater making it a delight to look at.

MATERIALS

Handspun – commercially dyed worsted tops
8 threads per cm – single ply
20 threads per in. – single ply

Commercial equivalent – Aran (thin)
4.5 threads per cm
11 threads per in.

Handspun yarn
4 separate colours have been used in this design as follows:

Main:			
red/white pulled tog	75/25 g	100/25 g	100/25 g
tan plyed	100 g	125 g	125 g
A:			
white/yellow pulled tog	75/25 g	75/25 g	75/25 g
white Wensleydale plyed	100 g	100 g	100 g
B:			
dark blue/green pulled tog	15/10 g	15/10 g	15/10 g
light blue	25 g	25 g	25 g
C:			
dark green/dark blue pulled tog	15/10 g	15/10 g	15/10 g
dark green plyed	25 g	25 g	25 g

Commercial yarn
4(5:5) x 50 g balls Avocet tweed double knitting (red) for main
4(4:4) x 50 g balls (cream) for A
1(1:1) x 50 g balls (blue) for B
1(1:1) x 50 g balls (green) for C

Pair each 3¾ mm (9) and 4½ mm (7) and 5 mm (6) needles

MEASUREMENTS

To fit bust 82(86:92) cm [32(34:36) in.]
Length from top of shoulders 58(58:60) cm [22¾(22¾:23½) in.]
Sleeve seam 44(45:46) cm [17¼(17¾:18) in.]

TENSION

18 sts and 28 rows to 10 cm [4 in.] on 4½ mm needles over st st.

ZOE

Special abbreviations

M – main; A – 1st contrast; B – 2nd contrast; C – 3rd contrast

FRONT

With 4½ mm needles and M, start at bottom right hand corner by casting on 3 sts and P 1 row.

Now commence inc as follows:

1st row Inc 1 st into 1st and last st.

2nd row Inc 1 st into 1st st, P to end.

Rep these 2 rows until there are 105(111:117)sts.

The side seam is now completed.

Change to A and work shaping as follows:

1st row (RS) Inc 1 st into 1st st. K to last 2 sts, K2tog.

2nd row P.

Work 6 more rows in A.

Keeping the inc and dec correct, K58 sts in A. Change to B, K to end.

(Remember to twist yarn when changing colour to avoid holes in work.)

Continue on 2 colours as set and work 13(15:17) more rows.

This completes the width of the garment.

Cont to dec at neck edge *but* now dec by K2tog on *each row* on other end.

Keep dec as set until 26(28:30) rows in all have been worked in the B shade.

Next row (RS) Knit across A shade sts and the 1st 6 sts of B shade.

Change to C and K to end.

Cont to dec *as before* until 3 sts rem. Cast off.

BACK

With 4½ mm needles and M start at bottom

right hand corner again by casting on 3 sts and P 1 row.

Now commence inc as follows:

1st row Inc 1 st into 1st and last st.

2nd row P to last st, inc 1 st.

Rep these 2 rows until there are 105(111:117)sts.

The side seam is now complete.

Change to A and work shaping as follows:

1st row K2tog, K to last st, inc into last st.

2nd row P.

Work 6 more rows in A.

Keeping shaping correct, change to B and K47(53:59)sts. Change to A and K the rem 58 sts.

(Remember to twist yarn when changing colour to avoid holes in work.)

Cont on the 2 colours as set, work 13(15:17) more rows.

This completes the width of the garment.

Cont to dec at neck edge *but* now dec by K2tog on *each row* on other edge as follows:

1st row K2tog, K to last 2 sts, K2tog.

2nd row P2tog, P to end.

Cont to dec *as before*, change to C and K to last 6 sts of B shade, K6 sts in B shade, change to A. Knit to end. There are now three shades on row.

Keeping to shades as set cont to dec, *as before* until 3 sts rem.

Cast off.

FIRST SLEEVE

Knitted throughout in M.

With 3¾ mm needles cast on 35(37:39)sts and K in K1, P1 rib for 10 cm [4 in.].

Change to 5 mm needles and inc 19(21:23)sts

Marl – Aran (thin)

SPINNING INSTRUCTIONS													
Wheel Ratio	3:1	3½:1	4:1	4½:1	5:1	5½:1	6:1	6½:1	7:1	8:1	9:1	10:1	12:1
'Feed in' in inches per treadle Z	½-¾	¾	¾	¾	1	1	1¼	1¼	1½	1½	1¾	2	2½
PLYING INSTRUCTIONS													
Per treadles per 18 inches	15	12	12	12	9	9	8	8	6	6	5	4½	3½

evenly across row.   [54(58:62)sts]
Cont in st st and inc 1 st at each end of every 6th
row until there are 80(84:88)sts.
Work straight until work measures
44(45:46) cm [17¼(17¾:18) in.].
Cast off *loosely*.

SECOND SLEEVE

As first sleeve but knitted throughout in A.

WAISTBAND (back and front both alike)

With 3¾ mm needles and M and with RS
facing pick up and K 71(77:81) sts evenly along
bottom edge. Work in K1, P1 rib for 10 cm
[4 in.]. Cast off in rib.

TO MAKE UP

Be careful to match colours.
Sew shoulder seams, leaving a centre opening
of 25(26:27) cm [9¾(10¼:10¾)in.] for neck.
Fold sleeves in half and place centre to shoulder
seam and sew into place. Sew in red sleeve to
red side of sweater and cream to cream side.
Sew side and sleeve seams.

·15·

Technical information

TENSION

It is essential to do a tension square. The importance of *always* checking your tension before actually knitting your garment is excellently illustrated with these two garments. Two knitters, each with the same yarn, needles and instructions, have managed to produce two completely different sized garments. Who was right in this instance is not really important. The important thing is what are you expecting from your finished garment when you first cast on. On looking at the illustration the answer could mean that one knitter would need to increase the size of her needle (remember they are both using the same yarn) to bring it to look like the larger size or, alternatively, the other knitter would need to reduce the size of her needle to bring her garment to the smaller size. The answer in this instance was that the larger size was wrong. The knitter needed to take into consideration the fact that she was naturally a loose knitter and therefore the garment would inevitably come out bigger. By reducing the size of her needles she would have corrected her looseness and ended up with the correct size. The tension square would have told her all this.

It does seem strange that intelligent knitters will work for hours and days creating a garment that is quite likely not to come out correctly. Would that same person drive a car for hours, even days, to end up in Scotland when they wanted to go to Land's End? Yet I hear triumphantly time and time again from the lips of such people 'Oh, I never do a tension square'. Please, knitters, do a tension square *every time* before commencing a garment. It will not take up much yarn, nor much time, and if we cast off the square and fix a label to it with comments, date and what we are going to knit and for whom – what memories we then have to go with those photographs!

To do a tension square

Instructions for any tension square will give only the number of stitches and rows need to form a 10 cm [4 in.] square. Accurate measurements are quite difficult to obtain using only this number of stitches as one would tend to pull or push work to make the square fit.

It is necessary therefore to cast on several stitches more than the number quoted and to work more rows. I always cast on 40 sts and work 40 rows, then cast off, unless the yarn is very thick, for then fewer stitches are needed and it is not necessary to add too many more. *Always* use the needles and work in the stitch pattern quoted, *not* just stocking stitch. If the instructions say Aran pattern or moss stitch then you *MUST* work the Aran pattern or moss stitch.

After casting off the square, press work according to ball band instructions. Now using a rigid ruler, not a tape measure, and working in the centre of the knitted square, measure 4 inches across the work and pin each side, 4 inches down and pin each end. You are now ready to count the number of stitches and rows *you* have knitted to make your tension square to see how they coincide with those on the pattern.

If you have too many stitches to your 4 inches then you must try and get them down to the number quoted in the pattern and to do this change to a finer needle. If you have not enough stitches, again change your needle, but this time to a larger size.

TENSION

Another remedy, if the tension difference is quite large, is to knit either a size smaller or a size larger in the pattern to the one you would normally knit. It would not be necessary to change the needles in this case.

However, do not leave the decision to knit either a smaller or larger size to guesswork. After you have counted how many stitches make your 4 inches, divide this number by 4, using a calculator if necessary, to arrive at the number of stitches needed to make 1 inch. Now add together the stitches required, after all the increasing has been completed, for the front and back of the garment and divide this number by the number of stitches which make up your inch. This will give you the overall size of the completed garment.

Note a difference of 1 cm [½ in.] in your tension square means an additional 9 cm [3½ in.] on a garment size of 86 cm [34 in.], therefore the extra time spent working on a tension square means the difference between a garment that fits perfectly and one that does not.

STAPLE LENGTH

It is very important that you are always aware of the length of the staple that you are working on.

Even commercially worsted or coloured tops must be checked for staple and fibre length. To do this either pull the roving – it will pull apart when you arrive at the staple length – or pull a few fibres from the roving and check by measuring the length of these fibres.

It is this length that your hands must work apart. If, for example, the staple is 2 in. in length, holding your hands at 1½ in. apart will mean the fibres will not pull out to feed onto the wheel. By holding them at more than 2 in. apart you will leave a lump in the middle of the yarn that is being spun because the difference between the 2 in. and the actual holding of the fibres is not being held under your control.

Carding two different lengths of fleece or blending two different lengths of fibres together will cause problems. If for any reason you do have to do this then by using a woollen spin and the longdraw method you will make a reasonably good yarn. A better way around the problem, if you do have a particularly delightful fleece at two different lengths and you need to use all the fleece for your project, is then to *cut* the longest staples in two to match the shorter staples and use it all together. Remember the fleece is always cut at one end anyway and after the first year hogg or hoggett it has been cut at both ends, so one more cut in the middle will not make the slightest difference!

COLD WATER SOAKING

Cold water soaking of all the fleece prior to spinning is very important – almost as important as those tension squares! – for two reasons:

1. For visual colour.
2. For pleasant handling.

I learned my lesson when I spun a lovely pale grey Shetland fleece, taking many hours and pains to do it, only to find when plunging the skeins into hot soapy water that it emerged a glowing white! The grey was peat.

After the soaking, the fleece will be so much nicer to handle. Who wants to fight the dirt anyway? Soaking in cold water will not remove the lanolin but will leave the fleece clean and manageable.

Wool is self-cleaning – simply plunge the fleece, say approximately 500 g at a time, into a bath, bowl or bucket of cold water. *Never* run the water over the wool as you will risk felting it. However dirty the water is on the first plunge, leave it for several hours. There are enzymes in the fleece which help to clean it and if you immediately change the water these will be thrown away. After two or three hours, gently move the fleece to one side and pour the water away – preferably into your watering-can for those houseplants – refill the bath and leave for a further four to six hours. Rinse and dry in the normal way.

BLENDING ON THE DRUM CARDER

Cold water soak the fleece. When dry pull into

Yarn types suitable for different needle sizes

Knitting needle sizes			Yarn types		
Metric mm	UK	USA	UK	USA	Australia
2	14	00	2-ply		
2¼	13	0		Fingering	
2¾	12	1	3-ply		3-ply
3	11	2			
3¼	10	3	4-ply	Sportweight	4-ply
3½	9	4	Double knitting (thin)		(5-ply)
4	8	5	Double knitting (thick)		6-ply
4½	7	6	Aran (thin)		
5	6	7	Aran or triple knitting	Worsted	10-ply
5½	5	8	Lopi		
6	4	9	Double-Double	Bulky	12-ply
6½	3	10			
7	2	10.5	Chunky	Extra bulky	14-ply
7½	1	11			
8	0	–			
8½	00	13			
9	000	15			

locks or staples and ease fibres out and feed onto the drum carder. Feed mohair separately onto the drum.

Blending can be done by pulling out one strip of the Wensleydale and one of the mohair and spinning together *or* breaking down the two separate bats into strips, mixing together and re-feeding onto the drum carder.

Good preparation of fleece is vital so spend 80 per cent of your time in preparation and 20 per cent in spinning.

Metric to imperial conversion

cm	in.	cm	in.	cm	in.	cm	in.
1	½	14	5½	27	10¾	39	15¼
2	¾	15	6	28	11	40	15¾
3	1¼	16	6¼	29	11½	41	16
4	1½	17	6¾	30	11¾	42	16½
5	2	18	7	31	12¼	43	17
6	2¼	19	7½	32	12½	44	17¼
7	2¾	20	7¾	33	13	45	17¾
8	3¼	21	8¼	34	13½	46	18
9	3½	22	8¾	35	13¾	47	18½
10	4	23	9	36	14¼	48	19
11	4½	24	9½	37	14½	49	19¼
12	4¾	25	9¾	38	15	50	19¾
13	5	26	10¼				

The above conversions are approximate.
One inch = 2.54 cm

Gram to ounce conversion

gram	ounce	gram	ounce
25	1	275	9¾
50	1¾	300	10½
75	2¾	325	11½
100	3½	350	12¼
125	4½	375	13¼
150	5¼	400	14
175	6¼	425	15
200	7	450	15¾
225	8	475	16¾
250	8¾	500	17¾

The above conversions are approximate.
One ounce = 28.35 grams

ABBREVIATIONS

(and American equivalents for British terms)

alt – *alternate (USA: every other)*
approx – *approximately*
beg – *beginning*
cable needle – *(USA: double pointed needle)*
cast off – *(USA: bind off)*
ch – *chain*
cm – *centimetre*
cont – *continue*
dc – *double crochet (USA: single crochet)*
dec – *decrease*
foll – *following*
g – *gram*
gst – *garter stitch*
in. – *inch*
inc. – *increase*
incl – *inclusive*
dec – *decrease*
K – *knit*
K2tog – *knit 2 together*
kg – *kilogram*
M1 – *make one stitch by picking up horizontal loop lying before next stitch and working into back of it*

mm – *millimetre*
P – *purl*
patt – *pattern*
psso – *pass slip stitch over*
rem – *remaining*
rep – *repeat*
RS – *right side*
shape top – *(USA: shape cap)*
Sl – *slip*
Sl1K – *slip 1 knitwise*
Sl1P – *slip 1 purlwise*
st st – *stocking stitch*
st(s) – *stitch(es)*
tbl – *through back of loop*
tension – *(USA: gauge)*
tog – *together*
WS – *wrong side*
yb – *yarn back*
yf – *yarn front*
yon – *yarn over needle*
yrn – *yarn round needle*

COMMERCIAL YARNS

England

Aero Needles Group plc (*for Schachenmayr yarn*)
P.O. Box 2
Edward Street
Redditch
Worcs B97 6HB
Tel: Redditch (0527) 67771/6

Emu Wools Ltd
Leeds Road
Greengates
Bradford
West Yorks BD10 9TE
Tel: Bradford (0274) 614031

Hammond Associates Ltd (*for Avocet yarn*)
Hammerain House
Hookstone Avenue
Harrogate
North Yorks HG2 8ER
Tel: Harrogate (0423) 871440

Richard Ingham & Co Ltd (*for Sunbeam yarn*)
Crawshaw Mills
Pudsey
West Yorks LS28 7BS
Tel: Pudsey (0532) 571871

Patons & Baldwins Ltd (*for Jaeger yarn*)
McMullen Road
Darlington
Co Durham DL1 1YQ
Tel: Darlington (0325) 381010

Priory Yarns Ltd (*for Georges Picaud yarn*)
24 Prospect Road
Ossett
West Yorks WF5 8AE
Tel: Wakefield (0924) 262137/8

Scheepjeswol (UK) Ltd
P.O. Box 48
7 Colemeadow Road,
Redditch
Worcs B98 9NZ
Tel: Redditch (0527) 61056

Sirdar plc
Flanshaw Lane
Alverthorpe
Wakefield
West Yorks WF2 9ND
Tel: Wakefield (0924) 371501

H.G. Twilley Ltd
Roman Mill
Stamford
Lincs PE9 1BG
Tel: Stamford (0780) 52661

Viking Wools Ltd (*for Samband Lopi yarn*)
Rothay Holme
Rothay Road
Ambleside
Cumbria LA22 0HQ
Tel: Ambleside (0963) 2991

Wendy International Ltd
P.O. Box 3
Guiseley
Leeds LS20 9PD

USA

Susan Bates Inc (*for Jaeger yarn*)
212 Middlesex Avenue
Chester
Connecticut 06412
USA

Erin International (*for Sunbeam yarn*)
59 Mallet Street
Dorchester
Mass 02124
USA

Fibrecraft, Judith Zausner (*for Sunbeam yarn*)
11 W. 37th Street
New York
NY 10018
USA

Kendex Corporation (*for Sirdar yarn*)
31332 Via Colinas 107
Westlake Village
California 91362
USA

Leisure Arts Inc (*for Schachenmayr yarn*)
P.O. Box 5595
Little Rock
Arkansas 72215
USA

Merino Wool Co Inc (*for Georges Picaud yarn*)
230 Fifth Avenue
Suite 2000
New York NY 10001
USA

The Plymouth Yarn Co Ltd (*for Emu yarn*)
P.O. Box 28
500 Lafayette Street
Bristol
PA 1900T
USA

Scheepjeswol (USA) Ltd (*for Scheepjeswol yarn*)
155 Lafayette Avenue
White Plains
New York 10603
USA

Shepherd Wool (*for Samband Lopi yarn*)
923 Industries Drive
Seattle W.A. 98188
USA

White Buffalo Mills Ltd (*for Wendy yarn*)
123 Third Street
Pembina
North Dakota 58271
USA

Canada

Diamond Yarn (Canada) Corp (*for Sirdar yarn*)
153 Bridgeland
Unit 11
Toronto M6A 2Y6
Canada

Estelle Designs & Sales Ltd
(*for Sunbeam and Avocet yarns*)
1135 Queen Street East
Toronto
Ontario
Canada

Fron Enterprises Ltd (*for Samband Lopi yarn*)
4160 Halifax Street
Burnaby B.C. U5C 3X2
Canada

Innovations CF Ltd (*for Georges Picaud yarn*)
338 St Antoine Est
Montreal
Quebec H2Y 1A3
Canada

S.R. Kertzer Ltd (*for Emu and Twilley yarns*)
257 Adelaide Street West
Toronto
Ontario M5H 181
Canada

Patons & Baldwins Ltd (*for Jaeger yarn*)
1001 Roselawn Avenue
Toronto M6B 1B8
Canada

Sheepjeswol (Canada) Ltd
400B Montee de Liesse
Montreal
Quebec H4T 1NG
Canada

R. Stein Yarn Corporation Ltd
(*for Schachenmayr yarn*)
Place de la Mode
5800 St Denis Street
Suite 303
Montreal
Quebec H2S 3L5
Canada

White Buffalo Ltd (*for Wendy yarn*)
545 Assiniboine Avenue
Brandon
Manitoba R7A 0G3
Canada

Australia

Coats Patons (Australia) Ltd
(*for Jaeger and Schachenbmayr yarn*)
P.O. Box 110
Ferntree Gully Road
Mount Waverley
Victoria
Australia

The Craft Warehouse (*for Wendy yarn*)
30 Gueos Avenue
Arncliffe
New South Wales 2205
Australia

Karingal Vic/Tas Pty Ltd (*for Emu yarn*)
Factory 2
359 Dorset Road
Bayswater
Victoria 3153
Australia

Oliver (Australia) Pty Ltd
(*for Georges Picaud yarn*)
47-57 Collins Street
Alexandria
Sydney
Australia

Panda Yarns (*for Twilley yarn*)
17/27 Brunswick Road
East Brunswick
Victoria 3057
Australia

Norman Ritchie Fabrics
(*for Samband Lopi yarn*)
607 Nicholson Street
Calton 3054
Australia

Sheepjeswol (Australia)
726 High Street
East Kew 3102
P.O. Box 99
Victoria
Australia

Sirdar (Australia) Pty Ltd
P.O. Box 110
Mt Waverley
Victoria 3149
Australia

Mrs S. Warner (*for Sunbeam yarn*)
39 Tennyson Street
East Malvern
Victoria 3145
Australia

New Zealand

Alltex International (*for Sirdar and Twilley yarns*)
P.O. Box 716
Dunedin
New Zealand

Coats Patons (New Zealand) Ltd
(*for Jaeger yarn*)
Mohuia Crescent
P.O. Box 50-140
Elsdon
Porirua
Wellington
New Zealand

Semco (New Zealand) Ltd
(*for Schachenmayr yarn*)
P.O. Box 50-290
Mohuia Crescent
Elsdon
Porirua
New Zealand

Thorobred (*for Scheepjeswol yarn*)
Scheepjeswol (New Zealand)
300 Richmond Road
Grey Lynn
Auckland 2
New Zealand

Wendy Wools New Zealand Ltd
P.O. Box 29107
Greenwoods Corner
Auckland 3
New Zealand

DYLON COLD WATER DYES

England

Dylon International Ltd
Worsley Bridge Road
Lower Sydenham
London SE26 5HD
Tel: 01-650 4801

Canada/USA

Farquhar International
939 Dillingham Road
Pickering
Ontario L1W 1Z7
Canada

Australia

S.T. Whitfield (Pty) Ltd
18-20 Punch Street
Artarmon 2064
New South Wales
Australia

New Zealand

T.A. Macalister Ltd
Private Bag
Auckland
New Zealand

SINGLE AND DOUBLE EDGED SATIN RIBBON

England

C.M. Offray & Son Ltd
Fir Tree Place
Church Road
Ashford
Middx TW15 2PH
Tel: Ashford (07842) 47281

USA

C.M. Offray & Son Ltd
Route 24
Box 601
Chester
New Jersey
USA

Canada

Offray
Suite 720
Westmount
Montreal
Canada

Australia/New Zealand

Butterick
P.O. Box 36
Lidcombe
New South Wales
Australia

FLEECES

British Wool Marketing Board
Kew Bridge House
Brentford
Middx TW8 0EL

Cotswold Farm Park
Bemborough Guiting Power
Glos

Jacob Fleece Society
St Leonards
Tring
Herts

Local Wool Staplers
Craftsman's Mark Ltd
Trefnant
Denbigh
Clwyd

HAIR FIBRES

Cottage Crafts
1 Aked Street
Bradford

DYES AND MORDANTS

London Textile Workshop
65 Roseberry Road
London N10 2LE

Matheson Dyes & Chemicals
Marcon Place
London E8 1LP

SEEDS

John & Caroline Stevens
Sawyers Farm
Little Cornard
Sudbury

GENERAL

Bodeilio Weaving & Craft Centre
Talwrn
Nr Llangefni
Anglesey
Gwyndd

Campden Weavers
16 Lower High Street
Chipping Campden
Glos GL55 6DY

Craft Technique
19 Old Orchard Street
Bath
Avon

Dryad
P.O. Box 38
Northgate
Yorks

Handweaver's Studio & Gallery
29 Haroldstone Road
London E17 7AN

Helios Fountain
7 Grassmarket
Edinburgh

Kineton Gallery
Banbury Street
Kineton
Warwickshire CV35 0JS

Little London Spinners
7 Tee Court
Romsey
Hants SO5 8GY

Elizabeth Palmer
Crown Cottage
46 High Street
Gretton Corby
Northants

Ruth Palfrey
South Hill Farm
Yeoford
Crediton
Devon

Shuttlewood Studio
Grange Cottage
Lion Walk
Beeleigh
Maldon
Essex
CM9 6LL
Tel: Maldon (0621) 55349

Spinners
Eileen Ringwood
Bricklyn Farm
Hoe Dereham
Norfolk NR19 2CR

Susan Foster
9 Windermere Road
Kendal
Cumbria

Textile Workshop & Gallery
166 High Street
Edinburgh

Wingham Wool Works
The Building Yard
Rotherham Road
Wentworth
South Yorks

OTHER USEFUL ADDRESSES

British Wool Marketing Board
Oak Mills
Clayton
Bradford
West Yorks BD14 6JD

Rare Breeds Survival Trust
4th Street
NAC Stoneleigh Park
Kenilworth
Warwicks CV8 2LG

Association of Guild of Weavers, Spinners
& Dyers
c/o Five Bays
10 Stancliffe Avenue
Marford
Wrexham
Clwyd

CoSIRA
141 Castle Street
Salisbury
Wilts

Crafts Council
12 Waterloo Place
London SW1Y 4AU

Federation of British Craft Societies
British Craft Centre
43 Earlham Street
London WC2

London Building of Weavers, Spinners
& Dyers
c/o Scotts Lane
Bromley
Kent

BIBLIOGRAPHY

Davenport, Elsie, *Your Handspinning*, London, 1953

Goodwin, Jill, *A Dyer's Manual*, London, 1982

Kiewe, H.E., *The Sacred History of Knitting*, Oxford, 1967

Ross, Mabel, *The Essentials of Handspinning*, Spinning Dale, Crook of Devon, Kinross, Scotland, 1980

Ross, Mabel, *The Essentials of Yarn Design for Handspinners*, Spinning Dale, Crook of Devon, Kinross, Scotland, 1983

Ross, Mabel, *Encyclopaedia of Handspinning*, Batsford, London, 1988

Ryder, Michael, *Sheep and Wool for Handicraft Workers*, Edinburgh, 1978

Shuttlewood, Nina and Biggs, Janet, *Designer Knitting from Handspun Yarns*, Batsford, London, 1984

Thomas, Mary, *Mary Thomas's Book of Knitting Patterns*, London, 1943

INDEX